THE TIMOTHY INITIATIVE

Disciples Making Disciples - Level 1
USA Edition

Edited by TTI Staff
18.6.20

This book belongs to:

_____

"And the things that you have heard from me among many witnesses, commit these to faithful men who will be able to teach others also."

2 Timothy 2:2

TTI Contact Information:

ttiusa@ttionline.org

TTI USA Website:

usa.ttionline.org

DMD Level 1 (USA Edition)
This edition published by The Timothy Initiative

For information:
The Timothy Initiative
P.O. Box 98177
Raleigh, NC 27624

Acknowledgments

We deeply appreciate and honor the countless TTI church planters and disciple makers around the world. Your faithfulness, commitment, and hard work are an inspiration to all and have been a key ingredient in improving this manual. Additionally, we would like to appreciate the editorial team who contributed directly to this revised edition: Fregy John, Moses Liancuh, Koudjoga Nenonene, Reji Dineep, Jared Nelms, Solomon Yero, Pat Robertson, David Nelms, Samuel Selvamony, Krishna Ghimire, Daniel Boro, Kevin Marsico, Matt Tumas, Kasey Channita, and the many others who contributed to simplifying and making this manual more practical. All gratitude to Tammy Randlett for her editorial efforts. Special thanks also to Chris Dunlap who is helping TTI USA make disciples and plant micro-churches, one book at a time.

We have been blessed by the following individuals and ministries for their godly character, leadership, insight, and inspiration, which contributed to the formation of this manual:

- Dr. George Patterson and Richard Scoggins' *Church Multiplication Guide*
- Curtis Sergeant, Ying Kai, and *T4T*
- Bruce Bennett and One Mission in South Africa for their *Mobilizing Members* manual
- Campus Crusade's *Prayer, Care, and Share* manual
- Dr. Alex Abraham & Operation Agape's Joshua Institute in Asia
- David Watson and *Discovery Bible Study* principles
- Nathan Shank and *Four Fields of Kingdom Growth* & East West for their 4 Fields design
- Jimmy Scroggins and Three Circles
- Todd Wilson's *More: Finding Your Personal Calling*
- Steve Smith's *Spirit Walk: The Extraordinary Power of Acts for Ordinary People.*

Table of Contents

Welcome, Introduction, and Mission
Disciples Making Disciples - Level 1

What is The Timothy Initiative?

The Timothy Initiative (TTI) is an international disciple making and church planting movement. TTI was established with the purpose to train and multiply disciple makers and church planters around the world.

What is the Mission of TTI?

TTI's mission is to advance Christ's Kingdom by multiplying disciples and disciple making churches around the world.

What is the Vision of TTI?

In obedience to Jesus and through Kingdom partnerships, TTI's vision is to see multiplying, disciple making churches in every place and people group.

Brief History of TTI

TTI was originally called "Project India," as India was where we started. It was not until 2009 that we settled on the name The Timothy Initiative. Since then, TTI has expanded across Asia, Africa, and the Americas. Today, TTI has planted tens of thousands of churches across 42 countries and is committed to continue training disciple makers!

Goal: To equip ordinary people to be empowered by the Holy Spirit and be involved in an extraordinary mission!

Core Values for a Disciple Making Movement

1.   **Kingdom-Focused:** It's all about the King of kings and His Kingdom, so we share the work and give God the credit.

2.   **Spirit-Led, Scripture-Based:** The Holy Spirit and the Holy Scriptures are our guides in planting multiplying churches.

3.   **Integrity First:** God values integrity ... so do we.

4.   **Disciple Making Leads to Church Planting:** The best way to plant churches is by making disciple makers.

5.   **Prayer Is Priority:** We pray throughout the process of planning and planting churches.

6.   **People Matter:** All people matter to God, so we reach out to everyone—large and small tribes, people groups, urban cities, remote villages, rich, poor ... everyone!

7.   **Faith-Driven:** We want to bring glory to God. If there is no faith involved, there is no glory for God.

These are the core values of TTI and part of what makes us unique. We encourage you to adopt them in your own life and ministry as you seek to raise up disciple makers who plant multiplying churches.

Training Goals

Chapter 1: The goal of the trainer is to instill in every disciple maker a passion to daily pursue a Spirit-filled life (untying and raising their sails).

Chapter 2: The goal of the trainer is to equip and motivate every disciple maker to recognize and respond in obedience to the opportunities God gives them to share their story. (The harvest is plentiful.)

Chapter 3: The goal of the trainer is to equip and empower every disciple maker to effectively share God's story.

Chapter 4: The goal of the trainer is to provide every disciple maker with a biblical perspective of their identity in Christ and how to see themselves as God sees them.

Chapter 5: The goal of the trainer is to inspire every disciple maker to passionately pursue a deeper relationship with God by making prayer a priority throughout their day.

Chapter 6: The goal of the trainer is to foster a hunger in every disciple maker to study God's Word, discern His voice, and apply it to their life.

Chapter 7: The goal of the trainer is to show every disciple maker how to create a daily routine of spending time in God's Word, hearing His voice, and immediately obeying what He spoke.

Chapter 8: The goal of the trainer is to explain the value of training the next generation by equipping every disciple maker to confidently lead a Discovery Bible Study.

Chapter 9: The goal of the trainer is to help every disciple maker have a biblical understanding of God and how they can best respond to every situation in their life.

Chapter 10: The goal of the trainer is to encourage every disciple maker to commit to living on mission and participating in a local body of believers.

Purpose and Expected Outcomes

The purpose of this manual is to train, mobilize, and multiply disciple makers. In doing so, the Gospel will spread at a fast pace! We believe every believer is a disciple, and every disciple is called to be a disciple maker. It is important to note a few key distinctives as you begin this training:

TTI's simplified working definition of a disciple maker is as follows: **A disciple maker is one who lives like Jesus and leads others to do the same.**

For those who like to amplify, **a disciple maker is one who faithfully follows the Spirit of God, lovingly obeys the Word of God, and intentionally invests in the expansion of the family of God by training others to do the same.**

The training in this manual is designed to produce the following outcomes in the lives of those being trained:

Chapter 1: Every disciple maker will experience a Spirit-filled life (untying and raising their sails daily).

Chapter 2: Every disciple maker will regularly share their story of how Jesus changed their life with people where they live, work, study, shop, and play.

Chapter 3: Every disciple maker will make disciples by regularly sharing God's story where they live, work, study, shop, and play.

Chapter 4: Every disciple maker will stand firm in the assurance of their salvation, that Christ alone is enough.

Chapter 5: Every disciple maker will experience a healthy prayer life directed by the Holy Spirit and God's Word.

Chapter 6: Every disciple maker will faithfully read and study God's Word to better discern His voice and have the courage to obey whatever God says.

Chapter 7: Every disciple maker will set aside time every day to spend with God that includes the reading of His Word, prayer, and responding in obedience.

Chapter 8: Every disciple maker will gather a group of new believers or "pre-Christians" to lead them through a Discovery Bible Study so they can begin to read God's Word, hear His voice, and respond in obedience.

Chapter 9: Every disciple maker will make decisions and choices informed by a biblical understanding of who God is and what He is like.

Chapter 10: Every disciple maker will become an active participant in a local body of believers who are committed to the purposes of Christ and His Church.

Basic Terminology for Level 1

- **Training Center:** A location where training, learning, and planning takes place (usually in a church building or home).

- **Paul:** The primary trainer and mentor. Pauls model pastoral skills while working with Timothys. Pauls intentionally help Timothys make disciples and hold them accountable to follow through to multiple generations.

- **Timothy:** A disciple maker and trainer. Timothys are accountable to their Paul and are trained to bring new believers to Christ, disciple them, and lead them to do the same. Timothys intentionally help these new believers (Tituses) make disciples and hold them accountable to follow through to multiple generations.

- **Titus:** A new believer who is specifically identified by a Timothy to be trained to be a disciple maker. Tituses are accountable to Timothys and are trained by them to bring new believers to Christ, disciple them, and lead them to do the same.

TTI's Philosophy and Strategy of Training

Philosophy

TTI believes learning and doing go together. Both should lead to training others who can then go on to train others. Likewise, obedience is a critical part of discipleship; they should not be separated.

With this in mind, all of the training materials produced by TTI are not merely for educational purposes; every disciple maker is expected to put into practice what they learn in their personal life and ministry. As we partner together under the leading and direction of the Holy Spirit, He will provide each of us with everything we need to bring Him glory and the lost to His Son, Jesus!

TTI partners with churches and leaders to start disciple making Training Centers. Typically, training happens either in existing church buildings or in homes where participants receive hands-on training on how to make disciples of Jesus, who will in turn make more disciples of Jesus. All assignments center on spiritual growth, evangelism, and disciple making. For those interested, Disciples Making Disciples - Level 2 offers additional training on establishing micro-churches.

Strategy

Train disciple makers to make disciples where they live, work, study, shop, and play. In this manual, every disciple maker is encouraged to immediately start meeting with and intentionally developing any new believer they lead to Christ. They are also encouraged to target believers whom they know are not making disciples.

- The training is Christ-centered and Bible-based.
- The training is relational and non-formal (mentoring).
- The training is intentional, simple, and reproducible.

6

- The training is often held in a local church or home.
- The training is obedience-based and can be applied immediately to the disciple maker's life.

Every Training Should Include

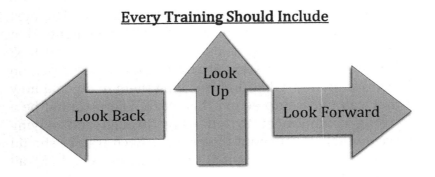

1. **Looking Back** gives everyone a chance to share about and listen to what is happening in their lives. This provides an opportunity for encouragement, celebration, and accountability. Looking back also allows challenges to be identified, course corrections to be made, and progress to be measured. Finally, it provides a chance to connect back to the core values, mission, vision, and purpose of the training.

2. **Looking Up** refuels our passion for loving God and others. Spending time in prayer and in God's Word provides nourishment to our souls and inspiration to continue forward. This offers a chance for each disciple maker to continue to learn and grow as Christlike leaders. Ministry is fueled by our relationship with God. Ownership of the core values, mission, and vision will only happen if we remain connected in relationship with Jesus.

   Hearing from God and responding to His Word is the primary aim of looking up. After each lesson has been taught, allow some time for prayer and reflection for each person to identify exactly what God is calling them to do. A simple way to do this is to invite God to speak to your heart and ask Him to show you the areas of greater obedience to which He is calling you.

3. **Looking Forward** offers a clear plan of action with timelines and expectations of what to do next. The next steps will be summarized with **"I will" statements** that bring clarity to what needs to be done before the next training. These next steps are based on what each person hears from God, what God is calling them to do, and how they can put it into action this week. There should be a strong commitment to following through and staying accountable throughout the process. Each trainer should make a note of the commitments made and hold all accountable.

Following the example of Looking Back, Looking Up, and Looking Forward will ensure that every training accomplishes the specific purposes, goals, and outcomes designed. This simple group structure, with this training material and a good trainer, will help every disciple maker grow in their **Beliefs, Skills, and Values.**

Beliefs, Skills, and Values

As a disciple and disciple maker, there are essential beliefs, skills, and values we should understand and develop to help us grow and live as mature followers of Jesus. We can define this simply:

- **Beliefs**: The biblical principles and understandings that develop a firm foundation, leading to a Spirit-filled, faith-filled, and loving lifestyle.
- **Skills**: The habits, patterns, and lifestyle behaviors we develop that help us grow and live as mature disciples and disciple makers.
- **Values**: The heartbeat and desires that reflect a lifestyle of obedience as mature disciples and disciple makers.

Every chapter in this book is designed to help us grow in our understanding of Scripture and how to apply those truths to our life. The "I will" commitments, assignments, and Looking Back and Looking Forward hold us accountable to grow as disciples and disciple makers. A good trainer with comprehensive training materials, good practices, and a reproducible process will help us become mature disciples who can be disciple makers.

Chapter 1 Trainer's Guide
The Spirit-Filled Christian Life

Training Goal (Heartbeat): Instill in every disciple maker a passion to pursue a Spirit-filled life (untying and raising their sails).

Expected Outcome (Skill/Habit): Every disciple maker will experience a Spirit-filled life (untying and raising their sails daily).

Look Back

Review the mission, vision, and core values of TTI.

Look Up

This chapter focuses on how to live the Spirit-filled Christian life, which is often referred to as victorious Christian living. As you train those you are discipling through this chapter, be sure to focus on these key concepts:

- Begin in complete dependence on the Holy Spirit and recognize that the Spirit of God is the foundation upon which this training must be built. With this in mind, train in a way that every disciple maker is depending on the Spirit of God in their everyday life.
- Emphasize how God is always at work and, without the Spirit of God, we are powerless and can do nothing.
- **Remember to highlight the expected outcome and key principle!**
- Encourage memorization of key Scripture verses.
- **Hearing from God:** At the end of this chapter, allow for a time of silent prayer and reflection, specifically looking for what each person should do in response to God speaking to their heart.

Group Discussion: Discuss how it feels to know that God is inviting us to partner with him in life transformation. How do you sense the Holy Spirit's prompting your actions, attitudes, and thoughts? How can you remain sensitive to the Holy Spirit's

11

leading as He connects you to people the Father is drawing to Jesus?

Model & Practice: Demonstrate how to untie and raise your sails. Share a specific example of when God used a small act of faith (raising their sail) to bring about an amazing encounter with someone who was being drawn to Jesus.

 ## Look Forward

Before reviewing the action steps for the chapter, pause and prayerfully discuss the following questions:
- How is God speaking to your heart today?
- How is God calling you to greater obedience?
- What will you do today and this week in response to God's voice?

*Remember, as you look forward, note what is said so that you may hold others accountable. It is helpful as each person identifies what they are planning to do to begin their statements with **"I will"** or "This week I will _____." Doing this will make the statements more meaningful and the follow-through more measurable. Every trainer should consider keeping an "I Will Journal" or finding another practical way to note the specifics so things are easy to reference from one week to the next.

Action Steps for this chapter:
- Write "I will" statements in the chapter journal on pg. 21. Make sure to share your statement with the group/trainer each week so they can hold you accountable.
- Begin each day asking the Holy Spirit to fill you—to take control of your life.
 - Memorize *Acts 1:8.*
- Read a chapter of Acts every day for the next 28 days.
- Ask the Holy Spirit to connect you with a pre-Christian this week. Actively try to identify who this person is. When you find this person, share with them how God's love has changed your life. **Be ready to report back to your trainer with whom you shared and what happened.**
- Under the guidance of the Holy Spirit, begin to make a list of potential pre-Christians (add their names on pg. 37).

Chapter 1
The Spirit-Filled Christian Life

Expected Outcome: Every disciple maker will experience a Spirit-filled life (untying and raising their sails daily).

The Importance of the Holy Spirit for the Disciple

In *John 14:16-17*, Jesus promised the Holy Spirit to His disciples.

"And I will pray to the Father, and He will give you another Helper, that He may abide with you forever—the Spirit of truth, whom the world cannot receive, because it neither sees Him nor knows Him; but you know Him, for He dwells with you and will be in you."

In this passage, we observe the following:
- The Father sent the Holy Spirit at the request of Jesus.
- Jesus described the Holy Spirit as a "Helper" and "the Spirit of truth."
- The Holy Spirit will be with us forever.
- Only followers of Jesus receive the Holy Spirit.

 Group Activity: Read *John 16:7-15* together.

This passage demonstrates that it is more important to be filled with the Holy Spirit than to be in the physical presence of Jesus.

Focus on *John 16:7-10*. Jesus also explained that the Holy Spirit will convict the world concerning three areas:
- The world's sin.
- God's righteousness.
- God's coming judgement.

13

In *John 16:13-15*, Jesus revealed that the Holy Spirit will be our guide and will lead us into all truth.

Be Filled with the Spirit

As the disciple of Jesus is led and directed by the Holy Spirit, it is important that they be filled with the Spirit. Knowing what it means to be *"filled with the Spirit"* is one of the keys to living a victorious and fulfilled Christian life. There are many truths about being filled with the Spirit that are important to remember:

- It is a command, not a suggestion.
- It is not something we do ourselves but something God does in us.
- We need to constantly ask the Holy Spirit to fill us.

The indwelling of the Holy Spirit and being filled with the Holy Spirit are not the same thing. The indwelling of the Holy Spirit happens at the point of salvation *(Acts 2:38; Romans 8:5-8; 1 Corinthians 3:16)*. Being filled with the Spirit, as commanded in *Ephesians 5:18,* means to be controlled by the Holy Spirit.

When you become a Christian, you get all of the Holy Spirit, but He doesn't get all of you. Being filled with the Holy Spirit is a process of giving Him control of our lives and submitting our will to His. We are either being controlled by our sinful desires or by the Holy Spirit *(Romans 8:5-6)*.

Untying and Raising the Sails

In order to live a Spirit-filled life, it is essential that you begin each day by asking the Holy Spirit to fill you—to take control of your life. A simple way to do this is by adopting habits that will prepare and remind you to follow the leading of the Holy Spirit.

In *John 3:8,* Jesus describes the Holy Spirit saying, *"The wind blows where it wishes, and you hear the sound of it, but cannot tell where it comes from and where it goes. So is everyone who is born of the Spirit."* If the Holy Spirit is like the wind, an easy way to understand what it means to live a Spirit-filled life is to think of our lives as a sailboat. Two things need to be done to a sailboat before for the wind can fill its sails:

1. You must untie the sails.
2. You must raise the sails.

Before a sailboat is able to leave the harbor, the sails must be untied from the main mast. By untying the sails, you are taking the first step to preparing the boat for its voyage. Our sins are like the ropes that keep the sails tied to the mast. Sin restricts us as we try to follow God faithfully. The sins we do not confess keep us from seeing the ways that God wants to move in our lives.

We "untie the sails" by confessing all known sin and surrendering our lives again to the Lord. By confessing our sins, we express our dependence and need for God to make us new each day and to prepare our hearts for the leading of the Holy Spirit. A life that is tied down by sin and our own desire for control will not be free to be filled by the winds of the Holy Spirit *(Hebrews 12:1).*

Untying the sails of a ship from the mast is not enough to leave the safety of the shores. In order for the sails to catch the wind, we must "raise the sails." When you raise the sails, you are opening your life up for the possibility that the Spirit will do something great with your obedience. By raising your sails, you tell God, "I'm available! This boat is Yours! Empower me and direct me to the people You want me to share my story and Your story with. Help me to better follow the Spirit, and to respond in obedience."

There may be days or seasons when you feel that your sail is too small to have an impact. Do not let this keep you from raising your sail and committing your day to the leading of the Spirit! God will do far more than we could ever imagine with small acts of consistent obedience *(Ephesians 3:20).*

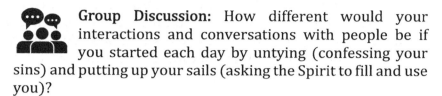 **Group Discussion:** How different would your interactions and conversations with people be if you started each day by untying (confessing your sins) and putting up your sails (asking the Spirit to fill and use you)?

Model & Practice: Untying and Raising the Sails
One of the action steps below is to begin each day by asking the Holy Spirit to fill you—to take control of your life.

Your trainer will take time to demonstrate how to ask the Holy Spirit to fill you by untying and raising your sails. Your trainer will share a specific example of when God used their small act of faith (raising their sail) to bring about **something** great in their life or the life of another.

After doing this, divide into smaller groups to practice. Identify one or two people in your group who can be your accountability partner throughout this training. Give them permission to ask if you are daily untying your sails (confessing your sins) and putting up your sails (asking the Spirit to fill and use you).

The Holy Spirit in the Process of Making Disciples

Jesus discipled His twelve followers for three years. The twelve lived and ministered with their Teacher, but He told them it was necessary that He go so He could ask the Father to send the Holy Spirit. He instructed them to wait in Jerusalem for the promise of the Father—the filling of the Holy Spirit. Why did Jesus want the disciples to have the Spirit?

"You shall receive power when the Holy Spirit has come upon you; and you shall be witnesses to Me in Jerusalem, and in all Judea and Samaria, and to the end of the earth" (Acts 1:8).

Jesus promised that His disciples would **receive power** when the Holy Spirit filled them. The purpose of being filled by the Holy Spirit was to empower the believers to be bold witnesses for Jesus. All throughout the Book of Acts, ordinary people were led and empowered by the Holy Spirit, which resulted in lost people coming to faith in Jesus and glory being brought to God. The same promise is true for every disciple of Jesus today!

 Key Principle: God the Father is constantly drawing people to Jesus through the ministry of the Holy Spirit. He <u>invites</u> and <u>expects</u> us to join Him in that process.

 Group Discussion: How does it make you feel that God is inviting us to partner with Him in this process of life transformation? How do you sense the Holy Spirit's prompting in your life through your actions, attitudes, and thoughts? How can you remain sensitive to the Holy Spirit's leading as He connects you to people the Father is drawing to Jesus?

As you journey through this training, you will be asked and held accountable to share your story (Chapter 2) and God's story (Chapter 3) with people where you live, work, study, shop, and play. Some of these people will be family, friends, or coworkers. Some will be complete strangers whom the Father is drawing to Jesus.

We call these people that the Holy Spirit is drawing to Jesus <u>pre-Christians</u>. They are all around us. The Holy Spirit desires to connect us with them. Are you ready? Are you intentionally looking for them? These people will often be used by God as relational "can-openers" to reaching their friends, relatives, and acquaintances with the Gospel of the Kingdom.

Sometimes these catalytic people are referred to as "persons of peace." (See *Luke 10* for this concept.)

Remember, one of the key roles of the Holy Spirit is to testify about Jesus. As you are filled each day, He will connect you to people whom He has already been drawing to Jesus. **Our strategies or unique gifts will not change the world; it is the fullness of Jesus in and through us!** We do not rely on our own strength and giftings but serve others out of the love that overflows from the Holy Spirit in us. Our dependence on the Holy Spirit is the key to effective living and evangelism.

Action Steps for this chapter:
- Write "I will" statements in the chapter journal on pg. 21. Make sure to share your statement with the group/trainer each week so they can hold you accountable.

- Begin each day by asking the Holy Spirit to fill you—to take control of your life.

- Memorize *Acts 1:8.*

- Read a chapter of Acts every day for the next 28 days. As you read it, meditate on the following statement:

"Every believer is a disciple, and every disciple is called to be a disciple maker."

What attributes do you see the disciples display in their lives and ministries?

- Ask the Holy Spirit to connect you with a pre-Christian this week. Actively pursue identifying who this person is. When He does, share how God's love has changed your life. **Be ready to report back to your trainer with whom you shared and what happened.**

- o You may need to ask the Spirit to fill you multiple times throughout the day *(1 Thessalonians 5:17-18)*.
- o Write down all you are hearing from God in your chapter journal.
- o Respond in obedience to what you are hearing.
- Under the guidance of the Holy Spirit, begin to make a list of potential pre-Christians. (Add their names on pg. 37).

Additional study for the month:

As you <u>read</u> one chapter of *Acts* each day this month, pay close attention to the lives of the disciples and how they live. Take note of how they respond to trials and the way they are empowered by the Holy Spirit. The disciples were ordinary, unschooled, and imperfect people, but because they were filled with the Holy Spirit and obedient to His leading, they could do incredible miracles. Take note that in every miracle you see, it almost always results in people putting their faith in Jesus! The disciples are great examples of who we should model our lives after and what we are called to do as we make disciples.

Make a list of all the actions and attributes of the disciples. Once you have a list, consider your own life and how you can grow to be more like them.

List the various attributes that you observe:

Read Acts
_____

_____

_____

_____

_____

Once you have your list, reflect on the following questions:

1. As a disciple of Jesus, how should I live?

2. Is there anything from the disciples' lives that is missing from my life? Give examples.

3. What behaviors, values, and adjustments to the way I spend my time need to change in order to become more like Jesus? Make a list and share that list with someone else.

Chapter Journal
This might be one of the most important pages in the book.

I will: _Ask the Holy Spirit to fill me_
daily
_____

I will: _____
_____
_____

I will: _____
_____
_____

I will: _____
_____
_____

Notes:
_____
_____
_____
_____
_____

Further Study: The Holy Spirit and the Life of the Believer

Read *Galatians 5:16-25.*

When we are living under the control of the Holy Spirit, He empowers us to live like Jesus. *Galatians 5:16* tells how **yielding to the Spirit will give us the power to overcome the cravings of sinful desires** (the flesh). This truth is the key to living a transformed life. The secret to overcoming our sinful desires is connected with being filled with the Holy Spirit.

Galatians 5:17-23 contrasts the differences between the desires/works of the flesh versus the fruit that comes from a life led by, and submitted to, the Holy Spirit.

Sinful Nature *(Fruit of the Flesh)*	**Holy Spirit's Nature** *(Fruit of the Spirit)*

Galatians 5:24-25 says that those who belong to Christ have crucified the flesh with its passions and desires and are called to live and walk by the Spirit.

- How have you experienced the filling of the Holy Spirit in your life this week? What impact has this made in your life?
- Ask: What ways do I see the fruit of the Spirit (love, joy, peace, patience, kindness, goodness, faithfulness, gentleness, and self-control) in my life? Explain.
- When we read the Scriptures, it is important to ask the Holy Spirit to help you understand its truths and how you can apply it to your life. Share an example.

Chapter 2 Trainer's Guide
My Story

Training Goal (Heartbeat): Equip and motivate every disciple maker to recognize and respond in obedience to the opportunities God gives them to share their story, (The harvest is plentiful.)

Expected Outcome (Skill/Habit): Every disciple maker will regularly share their story of how Jesus changed their life with people where they live, work, study, shop, and play.

 ## Look Back

Give everyone a chance to share, hear from others, and be held accountable. Focus on encouragement, celebration, and following through with assignments.

- **Obedience:** Have <u>everyone</u> report about how they followed through with their "I will" statements and action steps since the last training. Did everyone follow through with what they said they would do? (This can be done as a large group or in smaller groups.) It is important not to move forward with more training if the previous training has not been put into practice. Intentionally and lovingly hold those you train accountable.
- Sample questions to ask when looking back at Chapter 1:
  o How did inviting the Holy Spirit to fill and control your daily life impact how you lived this week?
  o Can you quote the memory verse – *Acts 1:8?*
  o Were you able to start creating a list of potential pre-Christians whom God placed on your mind? How many are currently on your list?
- **Review:** Go over the expected outcome and key principle from Chapter 1. Summarize the key points learned from the previous training.

- **Remind**: Training is for trainers. Everything learned should be put into practice. It should also be trained to the next generation.

 ## Look Up

This chapter focuses on sharing "My Story." As you train those you are discipling through this chapter, be sure to focus on these key concepts:
- Train in a way that every disciple maker is able to share their personal story of how Jesus changed their life. (During each training as you look back, allow time for people to practice sharing their story so they become more comfortable with sharing in front of others.)
- Emphasize how every believer is called to be a disciple, and every disciple is called to be a disciple maker.
- **Remember to highlight the expected outcome and key principle!**
- Encourage memorization of key Scripture verses.
- **Hearing from God:** At the end of each chapter, allow for a time of silent prayer and reflection, specifically looking for what each person should do in response to God speaking to their heart.

Group Activity: Encourage discussion as you introduce the four biblical principles that motivate us to share the Gospel. Divide into four groups and assign a verse to each group. Let each group report back on their findings.

Model & Practice: Demonstrate how to share the story of how Jesus changed their life. Show how to start a spiritual conversation using questions and "defining moments." Everyone else should also practice writing and telling their story, both individually and in small groups. Give everyone a chance to share!

 ## Look Forward

Before reviewing the action steps for the chapter, pause and prayerfully discuss the following questions:
- How is God speaking to your heart today?
- How is God calling you to greater obedience?
- What will you do today in response to God's voice? Have each person share their "I will" statement.

Action Steps for this chapter:
- Write new "I will" statements in your chapter journal. What will you do today and this week in response to God's voice?
- **After you have prepared your story, pray, go, listen, and share!** Take bold steps of faith! Ask for God's passion to reach the lost. Ask the Holy Spirit to also lead you to pre-Christians.
- **During the week:** Intentionally share your story with at least one person from the list of names you made on pg. 37 (and any other pre-Christians you encounter). Be ready to report back to your trainer with whom you shared your story and what happened.
- **Communicate with your accountability partner your plans, including with whom, when, where, and how you will share your story this week.**

Chapter 2
My Story

Expected Outcome: Every disciple maker will regularly share their story of how Jesus changed their life with people where they live, work, study, shop, and play.

As a Christ-follower, you are a child of God and a member of God's family. You can pray directly to, have fellowship with, and spend time with God at any time. You are an ambassador for Christ *(2 Corinthians 5:20)*. The Great Commission calls you to spread the Gospel and teach others to obey all of God's ways *(Matthew 28:19-20)*. Every believer, every member of the body of Christ, is to contribute to the growth and building up of the Church. We are all called to share the Good News of salvation: the Gospel!

 Key Principle: Every believer is called to be a disciple, and every disciple is called to be a disciple maker.

There are four biblical principles that motivate us and demonstrate the urgency to share the Gospel:

1. **The commandment of the Lord Jesus:** *"Go into all the world and preach the gospel to every creature" (Mark 16:15).*

2. **The reality of eternal separation from God:** A rich man's plea to share the Gospel with his family: *"I beg you therefore, father, that you would send him to my father's house, for I have five brothers, that he may testify to them, lest they also come to this place of torment" (Luke 16:27-28).*

3. **The personal desire to share the Gospel because my life has been transformed:** When the disciples were

threatened by the Pharisees to stop talking about Jesus, they responded, *"We cannot but speak the things which we have seen and heard"* (Acts 4:20; 1 Corinthians 9:16-17; Acts 9:16).

4. **The Holy Spirit's prompting and directing to those who are ready to receive the Gospel:** *"Come over to Macedonia and help us"* (Acts 16:9). The Apostle Paul's passion for reaching the lost compelled him to go.

 Group Discussion: Which one of the four principles impacts or motivates you most? Break into small groups and share with each other.

Imagine there is a disease that is incurable, and many people are dying daily. You repeatedly hear news about the hopelessness of this disease. Now, imagine that someone developed a cure for this disease and chose not to give it to everyone. What will the affected and infected people think of this person? **How would they feel if they knew healing was available, but they could not access the cure?** Thank God we have the cure! It is Jesus!

We should not only lead people to become Christ-followers but also to become disciple makers. By multiplying disciple makers, you can rapidly spread the Gospel. Unfortunately, most Christians think it is the job of professional ministers (for example, the evangelist, pastor, and missionary) to proclaim the Gospel. Most Christians consider "evangelism" to be inviting people to church and hoping the pastor will lead them to give their lives to Christ. **This is not God's design! Every Christ-follower should regularly experience the immense joy of sharing the love of God with others!** Bringing others to Jesus is the call of every disciple! Every member of the body of Christ is a minister!

Consider the verse from which The Timothy Initiative gets its name: *"And the things that you have heard from me among many witnesses, commit these to faithful men who will be able to teach others also"* (2 Timothy 2:2).

Every Christ-follower can and should share their story of how Jesus transformed their life with their neighbors, friends, family, and network of relationships. God always honors obedience and faithfulness to His Word.

 Group Discussion: Why do you think people do not share their stories of how Jesus changed their life?

Most Christians do not share their story or the Gospel for a few reasons:

1. **They are afraid.** The One with all authority in heaven and on earth is with us and promises never to leave us as we make disciples in obedience to His command *(Matthew 28:19-20).*

2. **They do not sense the urgency of sharing the Gospel.** Across the world, nearly one person every second is dying without knowing the possibility of eternal life in Jesus *(John 4:21-38).*

3. **They do not see people the way Jesus sees them.** Their love for Jesus has not compelled their hearts enough to love others and to see people the way Jesus does *(Matthew 9:36; 1 Corinthians 9:16-17; 2 Corinthians 5:14).* You may also feel like you do not know with whom to share. Taking the time to consider who needs to hear the Gospel is a simple but important task. In the next few pages, you will have a chance to consider with whom you can share.

4. **They do not know how to share the Gospel.** If this describes you, begin by asking the Holy Spirit to empower you to love God, to love others, and to lead and guide your life and ministry *(Romans 8:9-11; Ephesians 3:16, 5:18; Galatians 5:16).* Some of the best people to share the Gospel with are people you see on a regular basis and have a personal relationship with already.

Group Discussion: As a group, make a list of all the reasons people do not share. Before moving on, identify the reasons you do not share your story. Share those reasons with the group and ask for their help to overcome those fears.

In *Luke 10:2* Jesus says, *"The harvest truly is great, but the laborers are few."* You are invited and have the privilege of actually being the answer to somebody's prayer. Do you realize that God is already working behind the scenes in people's lives all around you, preparing their hearts to respond to the Gospel? Are you ready to partner with the Holy Spirit and be a part of transforming lives for eternity?

It is clear that you should share the hope of the Gospel with your neighbors, friends, family, and network of relationships. This is why we want to train you in how to effectively do this.

The Power of "My Story"
A well-crafted story of life change is incredibly powerful. In our culture of tolerance and acceptance of people's differences, your story can be an open door to start a spiritual conversation. Sharing a story can be an easier way to share a truth without it being offensive because it is difficult to argue with someone else's experience. Information will rarely inspire, but a story can connect and create a desire to hear more.

The goal of this chapter is to write a clear, concise, and effective story you can share with those to whom you want to present the Gospel.

The Basic Form of a Testimony
In order to help you have greater confidence in sharing your story, this basic outline can help you get started. It will help you be better prepared when the Holy Spirit opens an opportunity to share your story.

As you start sharing your story, there are some very important things that can help your story land on more fertile ground. Here are key aspects of effectively sharing your story:

Care	Prayer	Share

 Care: People won't care what you have to say until they first see how much you care for them. For this reason, it is important to show genuine interest in them and what is going on in their life. If you do not naturally care for and take a genuine interest in others, consider starting now. Ask the Holy Spirit to help you see people through His eyes.

 Prayer: Once you hear the needs and concerns of a person, ask them if you can pray for them. You might be surprised that most people will gladly let you pray for them on the spot. This can be an effective way to begin a spiritual conversation.

If you are not consistently praying for others, consider starting by practicing the three steps below:

1. Pray daily for your list of people who are pre-Christians (pg. 37).
2. Pray for boldness and awareness to share with those whom God brings on your path each day.
3. Be prepared to pray for others as you discover their needs.

Share: The purpose of sharing our story with people is to point them to Jesus and to tell them of the life change we have found through a relationship with Him. We share our story so others can have the same relationship with Jesus!

Writing Your Story

When you do share your story, it is best to organize your story around **three distinct parts.** This is the same format that the Apostle Paul followed in *Acts 22 and 26*.

1. **Before knowing Christ:** How I lived and what my life was like before I believed in Jesus. (If you came to Jesus at an early age, start with how Jesus found you.)

2. **Knowing Christ:** How Jesus found me (or how I recommitted or rededicated to an earlier decision).

3. **After knowing Christ:** How my life has changed because of Jesus.

It is important to craft your story intentionally so that it will connect with a lost person and help them see how Jesus transformed your life.

Model & Practice: Sharing Your Story

 Group Activity: Now your trainer will model for you how to share your story by using the outline below as a framework.

Step 1: Take ten minutes to write a rough draft of your story using this as an outline. *(The goal is to be able to share your story in two to three minutes. Make sure you give equal time to before and after.)*

My life before Christ: *(Struggles, brokenness, pain, pursuits, dysfunctions, emptiness, etc.)*

How I came to know Christ: *(How Jesus found me, or, what led me to put my trust in Jesus.)*

How my life has changed after coming to Christ: *(How Jesus has transformed my brokenness, pain, emptiness, etc.)*

After writing your rough draft, break into groups of two or three, and share your stories with each other. Choose your words carefully and assume that the person you are sharing with does not have a church background. Give feedback to help each other make it understandable to an unbeliever.

Step 2: Go back and look at the story you wrote down. What are a few key words that describe who you were before you met Christ? Write these words down as bullet points on the chart below. Some examples may include addicted, no purpose, lonely, empty, anxious, hopeless, angry, disconnected, abusive/abused, etc.

How has your life in these areas been transformed since you began a relationship with Jesus? For example: I was addicted; now I am sober. I was empty; now I am filled. I had no purpose; now I have meaning. I was alone; now I belong to my church family.

Connect who you were before Christ with who you are now, after Christ, to **show the change that Jesus has made in your life.** Add these to your story to be able to share what Christ has done in your life.

Life Before Christ	Life After Christ

Break into groups again with two or three people who have not heard your story. Share your story with one another and give feedback to help each other to make it clear and concise. As time permits, have different people share their story in front of the whole group.

*Once you finish practicing, write down the best version of your story on the next page.

Sharing your story is one of the most important tools in evangelism and is required as you go forward in this training.

*As you begin each chapter for the rest of this manual, you will be reminded to share your story. Sharing your story is so important that we recommend you select one or two people to practice sharing your story with before each training session.

My Story (Final Version)

My life before Christ: *(Struggles, brokenness, pain, pursuits, dysfunctions, emptiness, etc.)*

How I came to know Christ: *(What led me to put my trust in Jesus.)*

How my life has changed after coming to Christ: *(How Jesus has transformed my brokenness, pain, emptiness etc.)*

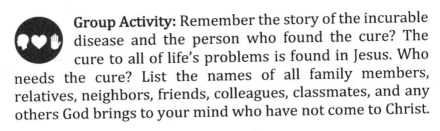 **Group Activity:** Remember the story of the incurable disease and the person who found the cure? The cure to all of life's problems is found in Jesus. Who needs the cure? List the names of all family members, relatives, neighbors, friends, colleagues, classmates, and any others God brings to your mind who have not come to Christ.

If you are struggling to think of 30 names, consider the categories below. If you are not sure if they are a Christ-follower, include their name.

List the first people the Holy Spirit brings to your mind:

List the people you call, text, and email most from your phone or from social media platforms (Facebook, Instagram, etc.):

List the people where you live (family and neighborhood):

List the people where you work or study (employment and school):

List the people where you shop (grocery store, restaurants, coffee shops):

List the people where you play (gym, sports leagues, teams, clubs, etc.):

My list I commit to praying for daily and sharing my story:

1. _____	16. _____
2. _____	17. _____
3. _____	18. _____
4. _____	19. _____
5. _____	20. _____
6. _____	21. _____
7. _____	22. _____
8. _____	23. _____
9. _____	24. _____
10. _____	25. _____
11. _____	26. _____
12. _____	27. _____
13. _____	28. _____
14. _____	29. _____
15. _____	30. _____

Action Step: If someone makes a decision to follow Jesus, ask them these questions: **"Who are three people you need to share your decision with today?** Who needs to know this truth about Jesus so they can also experience a relationship with Jesus as well?" Ask them to make a commitment to share it with them today or set up a time to share it with them this week.**

Consider these three blessings as you begin sharing your story:
1. It is a great blessing to lead someone to the Lord.
2. It is a greater blessing to disciple them and plant a church with them.
3. It is the greatest blessing to equip them to lead others to Jesus and help them plant disciple making churches.

Model & Practice: Starting a Spiritual Conversation

Your trainer will role-play how to start a spiritual conversation with someone in the group. First, the trainer will use questions to begin praying for someone. Then, they will use a "defining moment" to start a spiritual conversation.

When you listen to someone share their story, **really listen!** The person to whom you are talking may have defining moments with which you can relate. The moments when Jesus met you in your time of trouble can be a connection point with the person hearing your story.

Do you know how to begin a spiritual conversation with people? The following offers some practical ways to bridge the conversational gap to share your story/God's story.

1. **Ask people how you can pray for them. Remember to actually pray for them!** Here are a few ways to ask people if you can pray for them:
   - "Is there anything in your life that I may be praying for?"
   - After listening to them, ask, "Can I pray for you right now?"
   - "I have been praying for you recently, and I was wondering if there is anything specific in your life I can pray for?"

2. **Use "defining moments" in your life to connect with other people who have gone through similar hardships.**
   A defining moment is a time in your life when you experienced significant pain/hurt/loss/fear (parents divorced, significant health or medical issue, loss of a loved one, financial stress, emotional trauma, problem in school, etc.). Those defining moments likely became a moment of growth in your understanding of God and your relationship with Him. As you drew closer to God, you likely experienced His grace, mercy, love, presence, and/or leading in new ways!

As you listen to the stories of others, your defining moments can become a bridge in the conversation to connect with the person.

Group Activity: List three defining moments from your life that you can use to connect with others during a conversation. Describe how Jesus met you in your time of need. What did you learn from that difficult time or hardship, and how is your life different as a result?

When someone is talking to you about a struggle that you can relate to, use a defining moment from your life to bridge the gap into your story and God's story.

-

-

-

*Important Note:** Feedback from TTI disciple makers around the world reveals the average person will have to share their story with 15-30 people for one person to receive Christ. Do not be discouraged as you work through your list if a large percentage do not respond immediately. Remember the three steps: **Care, Prayer**, and **Share**. Continue in relationship with them, and you may have the chance to invite them to the group you currently attend or begin a Discovery Bible Study with them (explained in chapter 8). Don't give up! Continue to pray for them and follow the leading of the Holy Spirit.

Action Steps for this chapter:

- Write new "I will" statements in your chapter journal. What will you do today and this week in response to God's voice?

- **Now that you have prepared your story, pray, go, listen, and share!** Take bold steps of faith. Ask for God's passion to reach the lost. Ask the Holy Spirit to also lead you to pre-Christians.

- **During the week:** Intentionally share your story with at least one person from the list of names you made on pg. 37 (and any other pre-Christians you encounter*). Be ready to report back to your trainer with whom you shared your story and what happened.

- **Communicate with your accountability partner your plans, including with whom, when, where, and how you will share your story this week.** Hold each other accountable, and if helpful, go together to support one another. It may not always work out perfectly according to your plans but persevere and be faithful to Christ's commands.

*Important Note: You will have opportunities to share your story with people who are not on your list. Keep your heart open to the prompting of the Holy Spirit in your regular daily routine. As you pray, ask God to direct you to those who are hungry for Him and open to His Son, Jesus. He may allow your path to cross with persons of peace not listed above *(Luke 10:5-9).*

Chapter Journal

I will: _____

_____

_____

I will: _____

_____

_____

I will: _____

_____

_____

I will: _____

_____

_____

Notes:

_____

_____

_____

_____

_____

Chapter 3 Trainer's Guide
God's Story

Training Goal (Heartbeat): Equip and empower every disciple maker to effectively share God's story.

Expected Outcome (Skill/Habit): Every disciple maker will make disciples by regularly sharing God's story where they live, work, study, shop, and play.

 Look Back

Give everyone a chance to share, hear from others, and be held accountable. Focus on encouragement, celebration, and following through with assignments.

- **Obedience:** Have <u>everyone</u> report back on how they shared their story and followed through with their "I will" statements and action steps since the last training. (This can be done as a large group or in smaller groups.) Remember: Intentionally and lovingly hold those you train accountable.
  - If some or many did not follow through with sharing their story, consider not moving on with a new lesson and instead spend time in prayer, practice, and planning, specifically identifying how each person will share their story this week.
- **Review:** Go over the expected outcome and key principle from Chapter 2. Summarize the key points learned from the previous training.
- **Remind:** All training is for trainers. Are they training others with what they are learning? Has anyone trained someone else how to share their story?

 Look Up

This chapter focuses on sharing "God's story." As you train those you are discipling through this chapter, be sure to focus on these key concepts:

- Train in a way that every disciple maker is able to share the Gospel by telling God's story using the two methods introduced (3 Circles and the Bridge Illustration).
- Emphasize the importance of listening to and caring for others. If you don't listen to others, they will not listen to you.
- **Remember to highlight the expected outcome and key principle!** Encourage memorization of key Scripture verses.
- **Hearing from God:** Allow for a time of silent prayer and reflection, specifically looking for what each person should do in response to God speaking to their heart.

Group Activity: Each person should practice sharing God's story until they are comfortable and confident (ideally in two to three minutes). Do not move on until everyone can share their story and God's story confidently and naturally using the 3 Circles or the Bridge Illustration.

Model & Practice: Present the Gospel by sharing God's story using the 3 Circles and the Bridge Illustration. Show how to master three crucial transitions to leading someone to Christ.

 ## Look Forward

Before reviewing the action steps for the chapter, pause and prayerfully discuss the following questions:
- How is God speaking to your heart today?
- How is God calling you to greater obedience?
- What will you do today and this week in response to God's voice? Have each person share their "I will" statement.

Action Steps for this chapter:
- Write new "I will" statements in your chapter journal. What will you do today and this week in response to God's voice?
- Continue praying daily for the people on your list.
- Begin memorizing the five verses in the Bridge Illustration from Romans.
- Share God's story with two to three people from your list this week. Try to use the 3 Circles or the Bridge Illustration when possible.

Chapter 3
God's Story

Expected Outcome: Every disciple maker will make disciples by regularly sharing God's story where they live, work, study, shop, and play.

In the previous chapter, we looked at how to tell **your story**. In this chapter, we will learn how to tell **God's story**. While there are many ways to tell God's story, it is important to help connect your story with God's story.

 Group Discussion: What are some ideas of how you can transition from sharing your story into sharing God's story? Can you think of any phrases the group could use to connect your story with God's story?

Remember, the goal of sharing your story is to connect with someone in a way that they are open to hear you share God's story. After sharing your story with someone, it is a good idea to ask them about their story (or where they are on their spiritual journey). After they share their story with you, a great way to transition to God's story is to ask them, *"Would you be interested in hearing how you could have a friendship with Jesus, like me?"* or, *"Would you like to hear about how Jesus can transform your life?"*

If they say yes, they are inviting you to share the Gospel!

In this chapter, we are going to equip you to effectively use a method called *3 Circles*. There are numerous variations to this approach, and you can adapt it as you see fit. The main goal is to actively and intentionally share God's story with others.

 Key Principle: God loved the world so much that He sent His Son Jesus, so that those who believe in Him will receive eternal life *(John 3:16)*.

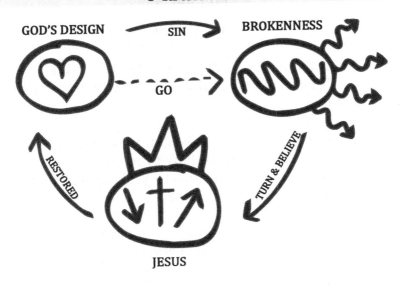

Sharing God's story is about having a conversation that centers on the love of God and His love for others. *(See usa.ttionline.org/resources/ for a demonstration of sharing God's story.)* Think for a moment how often you have conversations where people share their problems or a challenge they are facing.

Using *3 Circles* can help you turn everyday conversations about the problems and challenges people are having into conversations about Jesus and the Gospel. It does not always happen this way, but God's story conversations often stem from listening to other people's stories first. **This is important because understanding and identifying where people are hurting or struggling is a great way to start the conversation.**

There are many ways people will go about sharing their fears, anxieties, brokenness, or emptiness. As you listen, look for an opportunity to pray for them and ask them if you can show them a picture that changed your life. If they say yes, begin drawing *3 Circles*.

Group Discussion: Talk together about some of the ways people share their brokenness and challenges in everyday conversations. How can some of these issues be a springboard to share parts of your story or defining moments in your life?

Circle 1: Brokenness

Most people don't need to be convinced that the world is broken *(Romans 3:10)*. Both personal and worldwide brokenness surrounds us. As you listen to the trials others are going through, it is important to try to identify what they have done to avoid, escape, or get relief from the problems they identified. Eventually, everything people do to avoid, escape, or find relief from their brokenness will lead back to an awareness of brokenness and emptiness *(Colossians 1:21)*.

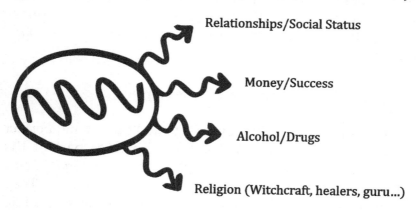

Relationships/Social Status

Money/Success

Alcohol/Drugs

Religion (Witchcraft, healers, guru...)

Keep in Mind: People often use relationships or substances to find healing for brokenness. They may pursue education, work, success, or money as a way to escape from life's problems. They may even try religion or modifying their behavior in an attempt to fix things.

The point here is to listen to their story and relate the circle that symbolizes brokenness to them (or you can share your story and how you tried to deal with your own brokenness).

Draw a picture based on the ways they have tried to deal with their own brokenness. This lets them know you are listening. The lines coming out of brokenness show the ways they have tried to deal with their problems in life visually. (The lines are like elastic cords; no matter how far away you try to get from brokenness, you will always end up back where you started. If they have not shared their story, you can share how you previously attempted to deal with your brokenness.)

Brokenness and emptiness are a result of sin, and any amount of sin separates us from God because He is holy. In order to have a relationship with God, we have to be perfect and without sin. **On our own, we fall short of meeting God's standard. This is why Jesus came to earth as a human: to set us free from our sins by taking the punishment we deserved.** Jesus wants us to be free and forgiven so he provided a way for humanity to be reconciled to God. Without Jesus, people have tried to deal with their brokenness and emptiness through their own efforts with no lasting success *(Romans 1:24-25)*.

 ### Circle 2: God's Perfect Design

The second circle to draw represents God's heart and perfect design. Brokenness was never God's heart or part of His perfect design. Ask them, *"Do you know what God's heart was?"* or *"Do you know what God's perfect design was?"* They may suggest it is changing our behaviors, going to church, trying to be good, or they may not have an answer.

God's heart for everyone is a relationship. When life was lived according to His design, it was perfect *(Genesis 1:26-27, 31)*. There was no death, disease, worry, fear, or anxiety, but we were deceived into thinking that we could be like God or there was something better than God's design for us.

When we disobeyed God's commands, we abandoned God. It was at this moment that sin entered the world. Sin is anything that goes against God's perfect design. As a result of sin, we became broken and empty. (Draw a line from "God's Design" to "Brokenness" and label it "Sin.")

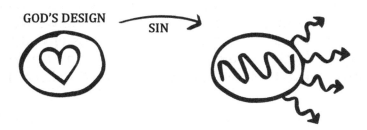

Bad News! This left us with no way to get back to a love relationship with God and His perfect design.
Good News! When we couldn't get back to God, God came to us.

 Circle 3: Jesus
The third circle represents Jesus!

 God sent His Son Jesus **down** (draw a down arrow) into our brokenness to die on a **cross** (draw a cross) for our sins *(John 3:16)*. He lived a sinless life and offered His life as a sacrifice for ours. Jesus became broken, humbled Himself, and became the perfect sacrifice for our sins.
Three days later Jesus **rose** (draw an up arrow) from the dead so that we could be restored into a right relationship with God and back to His perfect design *(1 Corinthians 15:4)*.

What is our response to Jesus?

 Jesus tells us to do two things: **turn** (repent) from our sins and **believe** in Him as the Lord and Savior of our lives *(Romans 10:9-10)*. When we turn and believe in Jesus, we submit to Him as King. (Draw a crown on the "Jesus" circle: He is the King!)

Jesus tells us to leave the sin, brokenness, and emptiness behind and promises to turn our brokenness into a new creation *(2 Corinthians 5:17)*. Jesus forgives us of our sins and sets us free from our brokenness and separation from God. Sin no longer has power over our lives as we are given a new identity and receive the righteousness of God through Jesus *(2 Corinthians 5:21)*. (Draw an arrow from "Brokenness" to "Jesus" and label it "Turn & Believe.")

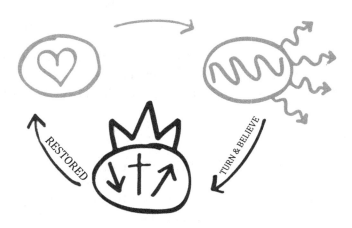

Jesus **restored** us to a right relationship with God, so we have the opportunity to receive God's love and grow in our relationship with Him *(2 Corinthians 5:17-18)*. (Draw an arrow from "Jesus" to "God's Design" and label it "Restored.")

With this in mind, Jesus tells us to GO back into a world that is broken and empty and share with others the love, hope, and healing found only in Him. By doing this, they too can turn from their sin and brokenness and enter into a love relationship with God *(Colossians 1:22-23)*.

We now have the ability, through the empowerment of the Holy Spirit, to live a life free from the bondage of sin. This is the hope we have in Jesus and the hope that others desperately need to experience for themselves. (Draw a dotted line from "God's Design" to "Brokenness" and label it "Go.")

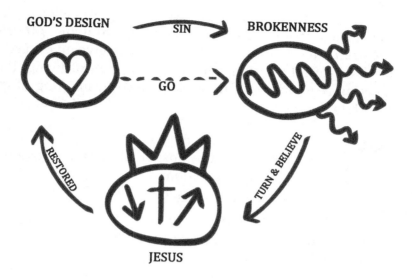

No matter how broken our lives are, there is hope for everyone! **When you get to this point in sharing God's story, ask if there is anything that is stopping them from making Jesus the King of their life today.**

After you share your story or the Gospel in any form, you can ask, *"Would you like to make Jesus King of your life now?"* If they say yes, lead the person to the Lord immediately. You can use the simple prayer below as an example. Remember, there is nothing special about reciting the words below, it is through faith in Christ that we are saved *(Ephesians 2:8-9).*

Lord Jesus, I confess that I am a sinner. I am sorry for all the wrong things I have done in my life. I believe and place my faith in YOU, that YOU came to this world, lived a perfect life, died for my sins, and were raised to life again, and through YOU, there is forgiveness of sins.

Jesus, I accept You as my Lord and Savior now. Please come into my life. I am Yours! Thank You for accepting me. In Jesus' name, Amen.

After leading someone in this prayer, encourage them to go and share what has happened with their friends and family. It is important to remember that we are not only called to share the Gospel of forgiveness but of Kingdom-living *(Matthew 28:18-20)*. Jesus is our King! We willingly give up everything we have to follow Him. This is a new way of living. Begin meeting regularly with those who make Jesus King of their life. Help them become a disciple who makes disciples.

 Group Discussion: As you consider the 3 Circles presentation of the Gospel, discuss as a group the following four questions.

- Why do I need to be saved?
- Why did Jesus have to die?
- What do I need to do to be saved?
- What happens when I am saved?

Model & Practice: Sharing God's Story

Your trainer will now take time to model exactly how to share God's story, answering any questions you may have so you can confidently share as well.

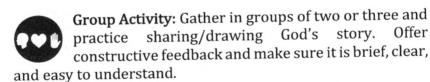 **Group Activity:** Gather in groups of two or three and practice sharing/drawing God's story. Offer constructive feedback and make sure it is brief, clear, and easy to understand.

- Make the Gospel personal by identifying their brokenness and revealing how God speaks into their pain with the hope of His Good News.
- Remove any religious or spiritual terms that people may not understand.
- Adjust the story according to feedback until it is clear and easy to understand.

Model & Practice: Mastering Three Crucial Transitions

One of the most difficult parts of leading someone to Christ is making these three transitions:

1. Going from a regular conversation to a spiritual conversation.
2. Going from your story to God's story (Three Circles or the Bridge Illustration).
3. Going from understanding the Gospel to making Jesus the Lord of their life.

Your trainer will now take time to model how to master the three key transitions to sharing the Gospel. Write any methods, key words, or phrases under each of the following sections.

- **Starting a Spiritual Conversation**

- **Your Story to God's Story**

- **From Understanding to the Decision to Make Jesus Lord**

Now, divide into groups of two to three and practice making these transitions. Give everyone an opportunity to role-play the person sharing the Gospel and the pre-Christian hearing the message.

* Alternative Option for Sharing God's Story *
The Romans Road

As mentioned above, there are a variety of ways to share the Gospel, and we want to offer an alternative and simplified version of God's story. Whatever is easier for you, we recommend using. **The main point is to introduce people to Jesus!**

The following method of sharing God's story is known as the Bridge Illustration or the Romans Road and uses another simple drawing. This is something you can draw as you share God's story. Begin by **drawing the following picture:**

Explain that the gap is man's separation from God.

1. *Romans 3:23: "All have sinned and fall short of the glory of God."*

   We all fall short of God's standard of perfection as our sin separates us from God. To sin means to miss the mark. If you try to throw a rock over a mountain, the attempt will fall short. Some will throw farther than others, but all will fall short. (Anything other than a bullseye misses the intended mark.)

2. **Romans 6:23:** *"For the wages of sin is death, but the gift of God is eternal life in Christ Jesus our Lord."*

What we earn for being a sinner is death and separation from God now and for eternity. This is why we need a Savior. Fortunately for us, this is exactly what we receive through faith in Christ. Forgiveness of our sins results in the free gift of eternal life.

MAN   GOD

Draw a cross to cover the gap.

3. **Romans 5:8:** *"While we were still sinners, Christ died for us."*

God knew that it was impossible for us to be without sin on our own, but God's love for us was so great that He sent His Son to pay the penalty of death we deserved. This means that He does not ask us to fix or clean ourselves up first in order to earn eternal life. While we were sinners, Jesus died in our place.

4. **Romans 10:9:** *"If you confess with your mouth the Lord Jesus and believe in your heart that God has raised Him from the dead, you will be saved."*

To make Jesus the Lord of your life means to invite Him to be the King or leader of your life. When we confess that Jesus is Lord, we surrender our desires and will to His. We acknowledge that His ways are true and better than our own. We commit our life to following and loving Him with all of our heart. Believing in Jesus means we no longer try to be good enough. Instead, we trust that Jesus died in our place and paid the price. It is now our joy and privilege to live out the freedom He gives us.

5. ***Romans 10:13:*** *"Whoever calls on the name of the LORD shall be saved."*

The Bible promises that those who seek after Jesus and call upon His name for salvation will be saved. Commit the following six verses to memory as a helpful aid to remembering the path to salvation.

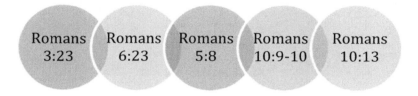

Romans 3:23 Romans 6:23 Romans 5:8 Romans 10:9-10 Romans 10:13

As people begin placing their faith in Christ, encourage them to immediately begin sharing their story. It is also important to lead them into a closer relationship with Jesus. Begin discipling them immediately.

It is good to follow every Gospel presentation with an invitation to accept Christ *(Romans 10:13)*. After you share your story or the Gospel in any form, you can ask, "Would you like to make Jesus King of your life now?" If they say, "Yes," lead the person to the Lord immediately. You can use the simple prayer below as an example. Remember, there is nothing special about reciting the words below ... it is through faith in Christ that we are saved *(Ephesians 2:8-9)*.

Lord Jesus, I confess that I am a sinner. I am sorry for all of the wrong things I have done in my life. I believe and place my faith in YOU, that YOU came to this world, lived a perfect life, died for my sins, and were raised to life again. Please forgive me of my sins.

Jesus, I confess You as my Lord and Savior now. Please fill me and transform me from the inside out. I am Yours! In Jesus' name, Amen.

Model & Practice: Sharing God's Story

Your trainer will now take time to model exactly how to share God's story using the Bridge Illustration, answering any questions you may have so you can confidently share as well.

 Group Activity: Gather in groups of two or three, and practice sharing/drawing God's story using the Bridge Illustration.

Make sure the presentation is brief and to the point.
- Offer constructive feedback to each other.
- Remove any religious or spiritual terms that people may not understand.
- Adjust the story according to feedback until it is clear and easy to understand.

Repeat this process until everyone is clear and confident on being able to share God's story.

Action Steps for this chapter:
- Write new "I will" statements in your chapter journal. What will you do today and this week in response to God's voice?
- Continue praying daily for the people on your list.
- Begin memorizing the six verses in the Bridge Illustration from Romans.
- Share God's story with two to three people from your list this week. Try to use the 3 Circles or the Bridge

Illustration when possible. Be sure to report back to your trainer what happens!

Next Steps for new believers/those seeking Jesus:

If someone has come to faith in Jesus or they are interested in learning more about Jesus, consider the following options:

1. Take new believers through the concepts of DMD in a relational way. *(You can use the chapter summaries at the back of the book to help.)*

2. Invite spiritually interested people to do a Discovery Bible Study with you. Start your own, or find another DBS for them to attend and go with them. (See Chapter 8.)

As you identify people who express an interest in spiritual conversations, try focusing more on connecting them with God instead of a set of ideas or truths about God, a church, or anything else.

Additional Resources: Linked below are free apps/websites that help you share God's story.

Go to <u>usa.ttionline.org/resources</u> for videos, articles, and other helpful resources to guide you as you go through this training.

3 Circles
<u>lifeonmissionbook.com/conversation-guide</u>

The Story
<u>thestoryfilm.com</u>

The God Test
<u>thegodtest.org</u>

Jesus Film
<u>jesusfilm.org/app</u>

God Tools
<u>godtoolsapp.com</u>

Peace with God
<u>peacewithgod.net</u>

Bible.is
<u>bible.is</u>

Romans Road of Salvation
<u>teenmissions.org/resources/roman-road-to-salvation/</u>

Dare 2 Share
<u>dare2share.org</u>

Chapter Journal

I will: _____

_____

_____

I will: _____

_____

_____

I will: _____

_____

_____

I will: _____

_____

_____

Notes:

_____

_____

_____

_____

_____

Additional study for this chapter: Understanding salvation
For a deeper understanding, let's answer four key questions about salvation: (1) Why do I need to be saved? (2) Why did Jesus have to die for me to be saved? (3) How am I saved? and (4) What happens when I am saved?

1. **Why do I need to be saved?**
   "For all have sinned and fall short of the glory of God ... For the wages of sin is death, but the gift of God is eternal life in Christ Jesus our Lord" (Romans 3:23; 6:23).

   God is holy and perfect *(Exodus 33:20; Isaiah 6:3).* It is impossible for an imperfect and sinful human to be in the presence of a righteous and holy God. We are sinners and the penalty for our sin is death and separation from God. There is nothing we can do to measure up to God's standard of perfection. This is why we need Jesus.

2. **Why did Jesus have to die for me to be saved?**
   "But God demonstrates His own love toward us, in that while we were still sinners, Christ died for us. Much more then, having now been justified by His blood, we shall be saved from wrath through Him. (Romans 5:8–9).

   God sent His son to take our sin upon Himself and pay the penalty for our sins by dying in our place on the cross. Yet, three days later, he conquered sin and death and rose from the dead. He has taken our sin and, in exchange, given us His righteousness.

3. **How am I saved?**
   "If you confess with your mouth the Lord Jesus and believe in your heart that God has raised Him from the dead, you will be saved. For with the heart one believes unto righteousness, and with the mouth confession is made unto salvation (Romans 10:9–10).

   Salvation is a gift. It cannot be earned. The way we receive the gift of salvation is through faith. When we confess our sins and place our faith in what Jesus did on the cross, we will be saved *(Romans 10:9)*.

4. **What happens when I am saved?**
The answer to this question is the focus of the next chapter. In your chapter journal, list some of the things that happen when you make Jesus the leader of your life. What things change in your life? How does your identity change? Your habits? Your struggles with sin?

Chapter 4 Trainer's Guide
New Identity and Assurance of Salvation

Training Goal (Heartbeat): Provide every disciple maker with a biblical perspective of their identity in Christ and learn to see themselves as God sees them.

Expected Outcome (Skill/Habit): Every disciple maker will stand firm in the assurance of their salvation, that Christ alone is enough.

 Look Back

Give everyone a chance to share, hear from others, and be held accountable. Focus on encouragement, celebration, and following through with assignments.

- **Obedience:** Have <u>everyone</u> report back on how they shared their story and God's story this past week. (This can be done as a large group or in smaller groups.) Have everyone share how they followed through with their "I will" statements and action steps since the last training.

- It is important not to move forward with Chapter 4 until everyone has put into practice what they learned in the previous chapter.
  - ○ **Do not move forward with a new lesson if someone did not share their story or God's story. Instead spend time in prayer, practice, and planning, specifically identifying how each person will share their story and God's story this week.**

- **Review:** Look back at the expected outcome and key principle from Chapter 3. Summarize the key points learned from the previous training.

- **Remind:** Training is for trainers. Has anyone identified who they are training yet? An easy tool to use to train others are the simplified lesson plans at the back of this book.

Before Looking Up, have at least two people practice sharing their story or God's story in front of the group.

 **Look Up**

This chapter focuses on our new identity in Christ. Be sure to focus on these key concepts:

- Train in a way that every disciple maker knows who they are in Christ and how to live out their new identity in Christ.
- **Remember to highlight the expected outcome and key principle!** Encourage memorization of key Scripture verses.
- **Hearing from God:** At the end of this chapter, allow for a time of silent prayer and reflection, specifically looking for what each person should do in response to God speaking to their heart.

Group Activity: Divide into groups and have each group focus on finding Scriptures about their new identity and the assurance of salvation. Give a chance for anyone who has not done so to make Jesus King of their life.

Model & Practice: Give personal examples of how you have overcome temptations, failures, fears, and hardships as a result of understanding your new identity in Christ.

 Look Forward

Before reviewing the action steps for the chapter, pause and prayerfully discuss the following questions:

- How is God speaking to your heart today?
- How is God calling you to greater obedience?
- What will you do today and this week in response to God's voice?

Action Steps for this chapter:

- Write new "I will" statements in your chapter journal.
- Memorize two verses from this chapter that speak about your new identity in Christ.
- Review the passages in this chapter. Write out key statements of who you are and reflect on how they should affect your daily living.
- Begin living out your new identity:
  - Learn to hear God speaking to your heart and obey His voice.
  - Ask yourself: *"How can I honor God most in this moment? What is He calling me to do?*

Chapter 4
New Identity and Assurance of Salvation

Expected Outcome: Every disciple maker will stand firm in the assurance of their salvation, that Christ alone is enough.

One of the most exciting parts about being a Christ-follower is knowing that you are completely forgiven and that you are filled with the Holy Spirit *(2 Corinthians 1:21-22)*. The Spirit is beginning to transform your life from the inside out. A key element of this transformation process is understanding who you really are now that you have a relationship with Christ. As you begin to understand your true identity in Christ, **it will transform your heart and mind so that you can become the person God created you to be!**

Take a few minutes to reflect on this short but important question: **Who are you?** This question is foundational to not only discovering your purpose in life, but it indicates how effective you believe you will be at fulfilling that purpose. The answer to this question is not what you do for a living or the title you tell people when they ask about your life. This question asks:

- How do you view yourself?
- What defining quality or characteristic informs your perspective and personality?
- What do you most deeply believe about yourself?

In one to two sentences, write down who you are.

_____

_____

_____

There are many ways to answer this question. It is likely that the culture or community you live in attempts to answer this question with their job title, social standing, gender, or nationality. While these areas are certainly *part* of our identity, they do not represent **all** of our identity.

Even though this is one of the most important questions in life for us to answer, we often neglect it. In order to help simplify the question, let's narrow the focus to one critical aspect of who you are. Which of these two words do you feel best represents who you are?

- **Saint:** *sinless, holy, perfect, righteous.*
- **Sinner:** *sinful, failure, imperfect, unrighteous.*

Where do you see yourself on this scale? Circle the option you believe best describes you as a person.

SAINT 1 2 3 4 5 6 7 8 9 10 **SINNER**

Why did you rank yourself the way you did?

_____

_____

Interestingly enough, the majority of Christians tend to identify themselves as closer to the "sinner" end of the spectrum than the "saint" end. As followers of Jesus, we know that we were sinners who fell short of God's standard of perfection and holiness *(Romans 3:23)*. As a result of this, it is very easy to become trapped in this mindset and focus on seeing ourselves through the lens of our imperfections and brokenness.

As followers of Jesus, however, we are also aware that Jesus came to set us free from the chains of sin that once bound us in darkness *(Romans 6:4-8)*. He came and lived a perfect (sinless) life. He willingly chose to pay the penalty for our sin by dying on the cross *(2 Corinthians 5:21; Romans 5:8)* even though He had done nothing to deserve the suffering and humiliation of death by crucifixion.

Jesus conquered sin and death by rising from the dead *(1 Peter 1:3-6)*. **When we put our faith in Him and make Him the leader (Lord) of our lives, something radical happens!** In Christ, we are completely forgiven, we receive eternal life, and our identity is forever transformed *(1 John 5:13-14; 2 Corinthians 5:17)*.

This radical change means we should no longer see our primary identity as *sinner*. Through faith in Christ and the indwelling of the Holy Spirit, we are considered "saints" (holy, righteous, perfect). Our identity has been transformed. If you circled anything other than a 1 (saint) on the scale above, you may be basing your identity on your performance rather than on what Jesus did for you on the cross.

 Key Principle: Your identity as a Christian is no longer based on your ability to meet God's standard. Your new identity is based exclusively on what Jesus did on the cross *(Ephesians 2:8-10)*.

 Group Discussion: Read *2 Corinthians 5:17 and 5:21*. According to these verses, who are you in Christ? Who have you become because Christ became sin for us?

As a follower of Jesus, you have been given a new identity; the old person you were is no longer who you are in this moment. When you surrendered your life to Christ, an exchange took place. Christ took your sin upon Himself as if it was His own. He paid the death penalty you deserved *(Romans 6:23; 5:8)* and in exchange, He gave you His righteousness *(2 Corinthians 5:21)*.

This is the good news of the Gospel of Jesus Christ! You are the righteousness of Christ. You no longer have to try to earn

God's favor. It was given to you the moment you surrendered your life to Jesus.

The New Testament is filled with over a hundred verses that describe your new identity in Christ. Read the verses below and make a declaration of who you are as a result of these truths:

*"But as many as received Him, to them He gave the right to become **children of God**, to those who believe in His name"* *(John 1:12).*

> According to this verse, I am a child of God.

*"I **have been crucified** with Christ; it is no longer I who live, but **Christ lives in me**; and the life which I now live in the flesh I live by faith in the Son of God, who **loved** me and gave Himself for me"* *(Galatians 2:20).*

> According to this verse, I am loved.

*"But you are **a chosen generation, a royal priesthood, a holy nation, His own special people**, that you may proclaim the praises of Him who **called** you **out of darkness** into His marvelous light"* *(1 Peter 2:9).*

> According to this verse, I am <u>chosen! I am royalty! I am holy! I am special to God! I am called out of darkness! I am called into His wonderful light!</u>

When the Apostle Paul writes to the churches in Corinth, Colossae, Philippi, and Ephesus, he begins each letter by confirming their new identity in Christ. Write down the word(s) that Paul uses to describe the believers in the passages below:

1 Corinthians 1:2
I am _____ .

Colossians 1:2

I am_____.

Philippians 1:1

I am_____.

Ephesians 1:1

I am_____.

In Christ, you are a saint, chosen, and considered holy because the righteousness of Jesus has been attributed to you on His behalf. **Remember the key principle above:** *You are not expected (and are hopelessly unable) to earn Christ's righteousness.* The Bible declares that you are already Christ's righteousness. You have a new identity based solely on what Jesus did for you.

Personalize the following truths about who you are by saying, "I am ..."

- The righteousness of Christ *(2 Corinthians 5:21).*
- A child of God *(Romans 8:15-16).*
- Forgiven *(1 John 1:9).*
- A saint *(Philippians 1:1).*
- Set free from the chains of sin *(Romans 6:6-7).*
- A masterpiece created on purpose *(Ephesians 2:10).*
- A joint heir of the Kingdom of God *(Romans 8:16-17; Matthew 25:34).*
- A royal priesthood *(1 Peter 2:8-10).*
- Chosen *(John 15:19).*
- Accepted *(Ephesians 1:6-7).*
- A temple of the Holy Spirit *(1 Corinthians 3:16; 6:19-20).*
- A vital part of the body of Christ *(1 Corinthians 12:12-14).*
- Valued and loved *(Romans 5:8).*
- A light to the world *(Matthew 5:12-14).*
- Given eternal life *(John 10:28).*

You now have the power of the Holy Spirit in you to begin helping you to be the person God created you to be. You have the privilege to now choose to live a transformed life empowered by the Spirit.

 Key Principle: The more you rely on the empowering of the Holy Spirit, the more your behavior will begin to reflect your true identity.

The Journey and Struggles of a "Saint"

Even if you know who you are and that the Holy Spirit has given you the power to live differently, you will probably still choose sin over God's glory at different points in your walk with Christ. Total transformation is a process, and it takes time to turn from your old ways of living and pursue Christ.

In this process of transformation, how should you respond when you sin? Recognize what caused you to sin: It's your old sin nature (old habit). It enticed you and led you to believe the lie that your sin would satisfy.

At the same time, you must acknowledge the sin you continue to struggle against. This sin has the potential to ruin your life and the lives of those around you. Sin separates you from God and holds you back from who God designed you to be. Don't stay in it. Here is a simple plan of how to respond when you sin:

1. **Responsibility** – Take responsibility for your sin, don't make excuses or try to hide it *(Psalm 32:5)*.
2. **Repent** – Ask God to forgive you. Then, turn away from your sin *(1 John 1:9)*.
3. **Reflect** – Think about what triggered you to sin and go back to your old pattern of living *(Galatians 5:16-21)*.
4. **Rise up** – Accept God's love and forgiveness (don't stay stuck in your sin). Get up with a greater passion, knowing that God has empowered you to live in freedom from sin *(Romans 6:4)*.
5. **Radical living** – Immediately start living out who you are in Christ! *(2 Corinthians 5:17)*.

70

Your Identity Is Connected to Your Purpose

"For we are His workmanship, created in Christ Jesus for good works, which God prepared beforehand that we should walk in them." (Ephesians 2:10)

You are God's masterpiece. Do you believe that? God made you on purpose, for a purpose. You are not an accident. He put you in your town, city, or community for a reason. He set you in this time period of history with the skills, talents, and platform to do great things for His Kingdom.

God is specifically designing opportunities for you to be a part of His Kingdom and mission. He is at work behind the scenes preparing people and opportunities for you to make an impact. If we are not living intentionally or are not sensitive to the prompting of the Holy Spirit, we will miss those opportunities. This is why we must live each day tuned to the Holy Spirit's voice, ready to obey without hesitation.

 Group Discussion: Read *Matthew 5:14-16.* Who does this passage say you are? What do you think Jesus meant when He said that you are the *"light of the world"?* How does this passage connect who you are with what you do?

You are the light of the world: Your attitude, actions, and the way you love and treat others should be so **radically different** from the world around you that you will stand out.

You have been transformed by God's grace: This is not just for yourself, but for the benefit of everyone you encounter. You are designed to display your light to the world; do not hide it from the people Jesus wants to save!

The disciples were 12 ordinary men whose lives and identities were totally transformed by Jesus. They counted the cost of following Jesus and chose to live radically different lives. Because of their willingness to do whatever God called them to do, no matter the cost, God used them to transform the known world in their lifetime.

 Group Discussion: Read *Luke 14:28-33.* What do these verses reveal about what it means to be a disciple? What is the cost of being a true disciple?

"A true disciple is called to immediate, radical, and costly obedience." - Curtis Sergeant

What stirs in your heart as you read the quote about what a true disciple is?

Are you willing to make a commitment to hear God's voice and immediately obey what He is asking you to do?

Take a minute to pray silently. What do you believe God is calling you to do? Share with the group what God put on your heart and how you are going to immediately put it into action.

Even though immediate obedience requires sacrifice and self-denial, it is the most exciting and fulfilling way to live. You were created for a purpose, placed in your city for this moment in history. It is impossible to imagine the unbelievable things God will invite you and empower you to do next! Jesus said, *"I have come that they may have life, and that they may have it more abundantly"* (John 10:10).

 Group Activity: Divide into seven groups. Assign one verse to each group and have someone explain how we can be sure of our salvation in their own words.

- *1 John 5:11-13*
- *John 5:24*
- *John 10:29*
- *John 17:1-3*

- *Jude 1:24*
- *Romans 8:16*
- *Romans 8:38-39*

72

What does Jesus promise to those who follow Him? In *John 10:28*, Jesus promises eternal life to those who follow Him: *"And I give them eternal life, and they shall never perish; neither shall anyone snatch them out of My hand."*

 Key Principle: If you have trusted Jesus to be your Savior and Lord, you have received eternal life. You have a new identity and are now a Kingdom citizen! Your service to the King starts now *(John 6:40).*

Our Assurance of Eternal Life

1 John 1:9 tells us, *"If we confess our sins, He is faithful and just to forgive us our sins and to cleanse us from all unrighteousness."* This means Jesus forgave all of our sins, regardless of when they were committed. If you are a follower of Jesus and you sin, you still have your salvation!

Your response:
- Has Jesus died for you? ____ Yes ____ No
- Have you placed your trust in Him to forgive your sins?
  ____ Yes ____ No
- Do you know you have received eternal life?
  ____ Yes ____ No

Possible Conclusions (circle/highlight one):
- I have become a follower of Christ.
- I haven't become a follower of Christ.
- I still don't know.

If you have made Jesus the Lord and Savior of your life, you can joyfully fill in your "spiritual birth certificate."

I received Jesus into my life to be my Savior. He called me, forgave my sin, took control of my life, and is my Lord. I have become a child of God, and I am a new creation. I have begun a new life.

Signature: _____

Date: _____

Model & Practice: Our Identity in Christ Informs Our Responses

 Group Discussion: Now that you understand your identity is founded in Christ, how should you respond to the following issues?

- When I am tempted, I...

- When I fail, I...

- When I am afraid, I...

- When I face hardships, I...

Your trainer will now give personal examples of how they have overcome temptations, failures, fears, and hardships as a result of understanding their new identity in Christ.

Action Steps for this chapter:

- Write new "I will" statements in your chapter journal.
- Memorize two verses from this chapter that speak about your new identity in Christ.
- Review the passages in this chapter. Write out key statements of who you are and reflect on how they should affect your daily living.
- Begin living out your new identity:
  o Believe what God's Word says about you.
  o Learn to hear God speaking to your heart and obey His voice.
  o Look for opportunities to be a light.
  o Live each moment asking yourself: *"How can I honor God most in this moment? What is He calling me to do?"*

Continue to share your story and God's story with two to three people this week. This is great news, and it is God's will. He is willing for all to receive salvation. Be ready to share what happens!

Chapter Journal

I will: _____

_____

_____

I will: _____

_____

_____

I will: _____

_____

_____

I will: _____

_____

_____

Notes:

_____

_____

_____

_____

_____

Additional study for this chapter:
After reading this chapter on your identity in Christ, what things has God spoken to your heart from His Word about who you are?

How can these truths transform the way you live? Be as specific as possible.

What steps can you take today to begin living differently?

Commit yourself this week to living out the Great Commission and the Great Commandment in the power of the Holy Spirit. This needs to become the normal way you live as a Christ-follower. In doing so, God will be glorified, and the Kingdom of Heaven will expand on earth.

- What is the main point of the Great Commission? Read *Matthew 28:19-20.*

- What is the Great Commandment? Read *Matthew 22:37-39.*

- How is obeying the second part of the Great Commandment evidence of your obedience to the first part?

- What is the most loving thing you can do for a person who does not have a relationship with Christ?

Chapter 5 Trainer's Guide
Living a Life of Prayer

Training Goal (Heartbeat): Inspire every disciple maker to passionately pursue a deeper relationship with God by making prayer a priority in their daily life.

Expected Outcome (Skill/Habit): Every disciple maker will experience a healthy prayer life directed by the Holy Spirit and God's Word.

 ## Look Back

Give everyone a chance to share, hear from others, and be held accountable. Focus on encouragement, celebration, and following through with assignments.

- **Obedience:** Have <u>everyone</u> report back on how they shared their story, God's story, and followed through with their "I will" statements since the last training. (This can be done as a large group or in smaller groups).
- It is important not to move forward with Chapter 5 until everyone has put into practice what they learned in the previous chapter. Remember: Intentionally and lovingly hold those you train accountable.
- **Review:** Go over the expected outcome and key principle from Chapter 4. Summarize the key points learned from the previous training.
- **Remind:** All training is for trainers. Are they training others with what they are learning?

Before Looking Up, have at least two people practice sharing their story or God's story in front of the group.

 ## Look Up

This chapter introduces how to live a life of prayer and devotion to God. As you train those you are discipling through this chapter, be sure to focus on these key concepts:

- Train in a way that every disciple maker is able to pray and have personal devotions with God on a daily basis. Encourage everyone to identify a daily time and place.
- Emphasize the importance of spiritual maturity, which requires regularly being with God, talking to God, and hearing from God. Especially focus on the model prayer of Jesus from *Matthew 6:8-13.*
- **Remember to highlight the expected outcome and key principle!** Encourage memorization of key Scripture verses.
- **Hearing from God:** At the end of this chapter, allow for a time of silent prayer and reflection, specifically looking for what each person should do in response to God speaking to their heart.

Model & Practice: Demonstrate how to use the prayer wheel as a model for personal daily prayer time.

 ## Look Forward

Before reviewing the action steps for the chapter, pause and prayerfully discuss the following questions:
- How is God speaking to your heart today?
- How is God calling you to greater obedience?
- What will you do today and this week in response to God's voice?

Action Steps for this chapter:
- Write new "I will" statements in your chapter journal.
- Commit daily to a time of prayer and identify who will hold you accountable. Make sure to choose a specific time and place.
- Every day this week, follow the model of Jesus by making prayer a priority. Pray 7 minutes a day, 7 days a week, for 7 people on your list. Specifically pray for their salvation and continue to share your story and God's story.
- Remember to take anything and everything to God in prayer at any time. There is no concern too small or need too large.
- Continue praying that God would connect you with pre-Christians and persons of peace *(Luke 10)* whom the Holy Spirit is drawing to Jesus. As He does, share your story and God's story.

Chapter 5
Living a Life of Prayer

Expected Outcome: Every disciple maker will experience a healthy prayer life directed by the Holy Spirit and God's Word.

To really know a person, you need to spend time with them on a regular basis. Regular communication is the key to any close relationship. It is the same way with God. If you want to have a close relationship with God, you will need to spend time with Him. In order to do this, it is helpful to "set a time" reserved for God on a daily basis.

One of the most effective and intimate ways to connect with God is through prayer. Prayer is simply "talking" with, "listening" to, and "hearing" from God. Prayer is communicating with God just as you would interact with a spouse or friend. When you pray, you should be authentic and sincere, modeling your prayer on how Jesus "talked" with God and taught His disciples.

 Group Discussion: Read *1 Thessalonians 5:16-18.* Based on this passage, what is God's will for your life? How often does He want us to pray?

It has been said that the heartbeat of the Christian life is prayer. If we aren't in regular and frequent communication with God throughout our day, we can feel spiritually "empty" or "dead." Prayer is also significant to living a Spirit-filled life. The Holy Spirit is in us and speaking to our hearts. We respond to Him in prayer and in obedience. We can pray aloud or silently in our head and heart.

Why Do We Need to Pray?

1. **Prayer is God's command.**
   - You should pray constantly *(Luke 18:1; 1 Thessalonians 5:17)*.
   - Pray in the Spirit, at all times *(Ephesians 6:18)*.

2. **To express our needs and concerns to Him:**
   - You can share all of your anxiety with Him because He cares for you *(1 Peter 5:7; Philippians 4:6-7)*.

3. **To seek God's leading and direction:**
   - *"Call to Me, and I will answer you, and show you great and mighty things, which you do not know" (Jeremiah 33:3; James 1:5)*.

4. **To receive and experience mercy and grace:**
   - *"Obtain mercy and find grace to help in time of need" (Hebrews 4:16; Acts 3:19-20)*.

What Can We Pray For?

*"Be anxious for nothing, but **in everything by prayer** and supplication, with thanksgiving, let your requests be made known to God; and the peace of God, which surpasses all understanding, will guard your hearts and minds through Christ Jesus" (Philippians. 4:6-7).*

Prayer is one of the most exciting blessings we receive when we begin following Jesus: We can pray to God about anything! God wants to fill us with His peace and wants us to experience joy in our lives regardless of our current circumstances.

This is the secret to finding peace and joy in our lives: Draw near to Him with your needs. There is nothing in our lives that God wants us to be stressed or anxious about and nothing that He doesn't want us to talk to Him about. He tells us to come to Him with everything.

Group Activity: Take two minutes right now and talk to God about **anything and everything** that you are concerned about now. If you feel comfortable, share those concerns with those in your group.

This week: Every time you sense stress or anxiety in your life, immediately stop and offer a prayer to God. Ask Him to extend peace to you as you offer gratitude and express your trust in Him to meet your every need.

10 Things to Include in Your Prayers:

1. Praise: Praise God's character and holiness. He is the creator and sustainer; He is all-knowing, all-powerful, loving, and truthful *(Psalm 147:5; Revelation 4:11)*.
2. Thanksgiving: Thank God for His grace, mercy, provision, protection, and salvation *(Philippians 4:6-7; 1 Thessalonians 5:18; Colossians 3:17)*.
3. Read the Word: Read God's promises in the Bible *(1 John 2:3-5)*.
4. Pray the Word: Pray through prayers recorded in the Bible *(Matthew 6:9-13; Colossians 1:9-12; Ephesians 1:15-23; Ephesians 3:14-21)*.
5. Ask: Ask God to meet your own needs *(Matthew 7:7-11)*.
6. Intercession: Ask God to care for and meet the needs of others *(1 Timothy 2:1; Philippians 2:4)*.
7. Confession: Ask God to forgive your sins *(1 John 1:9; Proverbs 28:13)*.
8. Listen: Ask the Lord to speak to you and respond in obedience when He does *(1 John 5:14-15)*.
9. Waiting: Be still; allow God to lead your thoughts *(Psalm 100:3; Psalm 25:5; 2 Thessalonians 3:5)*.
10. Hearing: Consider the things you have heard from God, and from Scripture *(1 John 4:16; Psalm 16:11; Psalm 23:4-6)*.

As you seek the Lord in prayer, there may be times when you are expecting an answer. In these instances, there are three possible responses from God: **yes, no, or wait.** God may not respond as quickly as we would like. We must be patient! Our response to God should be trust and obedience. We can be confident that He hears our prayers and cares deeply about us. We must also trust that He is strong enough to intervene and wise enough to know when to respond.

Five Keys for Effective Prayer:

1. **Pray "in Jesus' name" according to the Father's will:** Only through Jesus can a person enter into God's presence *(John 14:6; 16:23)*. Praying in Jesus' name is not merely saying the words, "in Jesus' name," but with a heart united with the heart of Christ. **Praying in Jesus' name is also a recognition of Christ's authority** *(John 14:13)*. Jesus has been given all authority in heaven and on earth by God *(Matthew 28:18; Philippians 2:9-10)*.

2. **Ending our prayer with "Amen" means praying with one's true heart:** Amen means "Let it be so." When Jesus taught His disciples to pray, He ended His prayer by saying, *"Amen" (Matthew 6:13)*.

3. **Pray in a conversational and authentic manner. Avoid "religious babbling":** It is important that our prayers are not meaningless routines *(Matthew 6:5)*. Prayer needs to come from your heart about what you are truly feeling, thinking, struggling with, and passionate about. Authentically sharing your heart with God brings Him great joy!

   David is described by God as a man after His own heart *(1 Samuel 13:14)*, and his prayers in the Psalms demonstrate what it looks like to communicate with God. He praises God, shares frustrations, and celebrates joys and victories. He apologizes for bad choices, shares his pain and sorrows, and acknowledges his utter dependence upon God in every area of his life. This is how we should pray!

4. **Pray anywhere, everywhere, and anytime:** One can pray at any time of the day and at any place—morning or evening, whether sitting, standing, walking, kneeling, lying down, etc. There is no limit on the time, form, and/or place of prayer *(1 Thessalonians 5:17)*.

5. **Pray with faith that God can do the impossible!** If there is no faith involved, there is no glory for God. Our prayers must be Kingdom-focused, rooted in God's Word, and faith-driven. All throughout the Bible, God does the impossible to reach the lost. In the Gospels and the Book of Acts, there is a clear connection between miracles and salvation. The fervent prayers of a righteous person are powerful and effective in "moving mountains" that are humanly impossible *(James 5:16; Matthew 17:20; 1 Corinthians 13:2)*. *"Without faith, it is impossible to please Him" (Hebrew 11:6; James 1:6-8)*.

Attitudes of Prayer

Attitude:	Verse:
In faith	*"But let him ask in faith, with no doubting ..." (James 1:6)*.
With the right motive and reverence	*"You do not have because you do not ask. You ask and do not receive, because you ask amiss" (James. 4:2-3; Matthew 6:9)*.
Confessing sins	*"Wash me thoroughly from my iniquity, And cleanse me from my sin" (Psalm 51:2)*.
According to His will	*"This is the confidence that we have in Him, that if we ask anything according to His will, He hears us" (1 John 5:14)*.
With perseverance	*"That men always ought to pray and not lose heart" (Luke 18:1)*.

Jesus' Example of How to Pray

One day, Jesus' disciples came to Him and asked Him to teach them how to pray. Jesus then prayed a short, simple, yet powerful prayer. We can learn principles from this prayer that will help us in our prayer life. Here is what Jesus prayed:

"In this manner, therefore, pray:

> *Our Father in heaven,*
> *Hallowed be Your name.*
> *Your kingdom come.*
> *Your will be done,*
> *On earth as it is in heaven.*
> *Give us this day our daily bread.*
> *And forgive us our debts,*
> *As we forgive our debtors.*
> *And do not lead us into temptation,*
> *But deliver us from the evil one.*
> *For Yours is the kingdom and the power and the glory*
> *forever. Amen" (Matthew 6:9-13).*

In this prayer, we can see at least eight principles that Jesus used to teach His disciples how to pray more effectively and sincerely:

1. Talk to God like a child would to their Father *(Matthew 6:9).*
2. Worship and praise Him *(Matthew 6:9).*
3. Pray for Jesus to set the world right and return soon *(Matthew 6:10).*
4. Focus on advancing His Kingdom and being in line with God's will *(Matthew 6:10).*
5. Ask Him to lead and be the King of your life *(Matthew 6:10).*
6. Ask Him to meet your needs and the needs of others you know *(Matthew 6:11).*
7. Confess your sins to Him and forgive those you have not forgiven *(Matthew 6:12).*
8. Ask Him for protection and victory over temptation and sin *(Matthew 6:13).*

86

Jesus shows His followers that prayer doesn't have to be long, complicated, or sound super spiritual. The most effective prayers are those that are honest, relational, and from the heart. God invites His people to bring every need, worry, or fear to His throne.

Model & Practice: Praying the Prayer Wheel
Your trainer will now take time to model how to pray through a tool called the prayer wheel.

The prayer wheel is a simple illustration that can keep you focused as you pray. It is also an easy way to train others how to spend focused time in prayer. The 8 key principles from the Lord's Prayer are represented in the prayer wheel below.

Praise & Thanksgiving
Principles 1 & 2

Confession
Principle 7

Intercession
Principles 3 & 6

Listen
Principles 4 & 5

Ask
Principles 6 & 8

Group Activity: Gather in groups of two or three and practice praying together through the prayer wheel. Begin and end your prayers with praise and thanksgiving.

Action Steps for this chapter:

- Write new "I will" statements in your chapter journal. What will you do in response to God's voice?
- Commit daily to a time of prayer and identify who will hold you accountable. Make sure to choose a specific time and place.
- Every day this week, follow the model of Jesus by making prayer a priority. Pray 7 minutes a day, 7 days a week, for 7 people on your list. Specifically pray for their salvation and continue to share your story and God's story.
- Remember to take anything and everything to God in prayer at any time. There is no concern too small or need too large. Stop and whisper a prayer as soon as any concerns come to your mind.
- Continue praying that God would connect you with pre-Christians and persons of peace *(Luke 10)* whom the Holy Spirit is drawing to Jesus. As He does, share your story and God's story.

The Gospel is great news, and it is God's will for us to share His story with others. He desires for everyone to experience it. Be ready to share with your trainer how God opened doors and gave you the opportunity to share your story this week.

Chapter Journal

I will: _____

_____

_____

I will: _____

_____

_____

I will: _____

_____

_____

I will: _____

_____

_____

Notes:

_____

_____

_____

_____

_____

Additional study for this chapter:

Prayer and Fasting

For those not familiar, fasting is simply choosing to go without food with a spiritual purpose in mind. It is not self-deprivation but a spiritual discipline for seeking more of God! While fasting, make sure not to allow your cravings to distract but to serve as a reminder for your need for Him and the spiritual hunger that people who do not know Jesus have every day *(John 4:31-38).*

Continue praying and begin fasting for the people on your list and for those you happen to encounter. Ask God to give you boldness, wisdom, discernment, and strength to help you be faithful. Ask Him to fill you with His love for the people you will be speaking with this week. As you feel the hunger pains, ask the Spirit to create an urgency to pray for and reach out to the people on your list. **Keep a journal of your prayers, and also note how God answers them!**

Chapter 6 Trainer's Guide
Learning to Feed Yourself

Training Goal (Heartbeat): Foster a hunger in every disciple maker to study God's Word, discern His voice, and apply it to their life.

Expected Outcome (Skill/Habit): Every disciple maker will faithfully read and study God's Word to better discern His voice and have the courage to obey whatever God says.

 ## Look Back

Give everyone a chance to share, hear from others, and be held accountable. Focus on encouragement, celebration, and following through with assignments.

- **Obedience:** Have <u>everyone</u> report back on how they shared their story, God's story, and followed through with their "I will" statements since the last training. It is important not to move forward with Chapter 6 until everyone has put into practice what they learned about prayer. Remember: Be intentional to lovingly hold those you train accountable.
  - Did you spend at least 7 minutes a day in prayer? Were you able to have a consistent time and place to pray?
  - Did you pray for 7 people on your list every day?
  - Did you practice praying about anything and everything? How did it go?
- **Review:** Go over the expected outcome and key principle from Chapter 5. Summarize the key points learned from the previous training.
- **Remind:** All training is for trainers. Did anyone train someone in prayer by using the prayer wheel?

Before Looking Up, have at least two people practice sharing their story or God's story in front of the group.

 ## Look Up

This chapter outlines a personal Bible study plan. As you train those you are discipling through this chapter, be sure to focus on these key concepts:

- Train in a way that every disciple maker understands the importance of growing in their love and knowledge of God's Word. Make sure they are also able to practically implement a personal Bible study plan.
- **Remember to highlight the expected outcome and key principle!**
- Encourage memorization of key Scripture verses.
- **Hearing from God:** At the end of this chapter, allow for a time of silent prayer and reflection, specifically looking for what each person should do in response to God speaking to their heart.

Model & Practice: Model how to do a personal Bible study so everyone sees how to do it. Practice together.

 ## Look Forward

Before reviewing the action steps for the chapter, pause and prayerfully discuss the following questions:
- How is God speaking to your heart today?
- How is God calling you to greater obedience?
- What will you do today and this week in response to God's voice?

Action Steps for this chapter:
- Write new "I will" statements in your chapter journal. What will you do today and this week in response to God's voice?
- Study the Bible using the SOAPS Bible study method at least one time this week in your devotional time. Be prepared to share what you have learned and whom you shared it with next training. Make sure to follow through on your "I will" statements.
- Follow up with those you have been sharing with. Encourage anyone you lead to Christ to study Scripture with the SOAPS study method you learned in this chapter.
- Continue sharing your story and God's story with at least two to three people this week. **Be ready to report back on what happens.**

Chapter 6
Learning to Feed Yourself

Expected Outcome: Every disciple maker will faithfully read and study God's Word to better discern His voice and have the courage to obey whatever God says.

A newborn baby relies on his mother to be fed, but he must eventually learn to feed himself. In the same way, Christians must learn to feed themselves in order to mature. One of the best ways to grow is to start spending time in God's Word on your own. As you begin trusting and obeying God's Word, allow the Holy Spirit to guide you through the following practices:
- Studying and understanding Scripture.
- Applying and obeying Scripture.
- Praying through and about Scripture.
- Sharing Scripture with others.

 Key Principle: Every believer must learn to grow in understanding, trusting, obeying, and sharing God's Word.

Knowing and obeying the Bible is a defining element in the life of a disciple. The reason we read God's Word is to hear God's voice and grow in relationship with Him. The more time we spend in God's Word, the more we will begin to recognize His voice. Once we hear His voice, we put what He said into action through obedience and application. This is why we encourage every disciple to read the Bible daily and read through it at least one time per year, every year.

Are you following a Bible reading plan yet? If you are going to make Bible reading a priority, you need a plan. Consider getting an app for your phone like the *YouVersion Bible,* which has a daily guide to help you read through the Bible in the next year. You could also buy a "Read Through the Bible

93

in a Year" Bible or find a resource online that can help you develop a reading plan. If you read just **four chapters** of the Bible every day, you will finish reading the entire Bible in 11 months. This means that even if you miss a day, you can read the Bible in less than a year. Ask your trainer if you have any questions about these or other options.

Feeding Yourself through a Personal Bible Study

A personal Bible study plan is a great way to be intentional and focused in your study of Scripture and growth as a disciple. The SOAPS process is a tool you can use as you learn to feed yourself from Scripture. **SOAPS** stands for these steps:

Scripture
Observation
Application
Pray
Share

Following these five steps provides a simple, practical, reproducible, and effective Bible study method that any follower of Jesus can use and train others to use. Let's describe this process.

Before you begin reading Scripture, practice communicating with God (prayer) by telling Him you want to spend time with Him. Ask that He speak to you through His Spirit and His words from Scripture.

Have paper, a journal, or a computer so you can take notes and record what you are learning, hearing, or processing as you study.

When ready, read or listen to the Bible and walk through the SOAPS steps as described below:

1. **Scripture:** Choose a passage and read or listen to it at least twice. Write down verses or phrases that stand out to you that you want to remember. Write down things you might want to understand better or have questions about.

2. **Observation:** As you read and re-read the passage, ask questions about the passage like the ones listed in the following bullet points. Write down your thoughts, ideas, or any truths you are processing from the passage.
    *   What did you like about this passage?
    *   Did anything concern you? Why?
    *   What does this passage teach us about God?
    *   What does this passage teach us about people?
    *   What does this passage teach us about sin?
    *   Is there an example to follow?
    *   Is there a command to obey?
    *   Is there an action to take or to avoid?
    *   Is there a promise to claim?
    *   With whom should you share this truth?

3. **Application:** As you are reading Scripture, think about what it means to obey these commands or concepts in your own life. Ask yourself, *"How do I need to respond today in light of what I have just read? What would I have to do? Is there an area of my life in which I need to do things differently?"* Write your thoughts and specific applications on what you sense you need to do because of God's Word and His Spirit.

4. **Pray:** Stop and think about what you have just read and sensed from this passage. Take a few minutes and ask God's Spirit to speak to you about any specific things you need to do in light of this passage. Write down anything you feel you need to do. Then, write out a short prayer that tells God what you've read in His Word, what you understand about obeying His commands, and what you plan to put into practice based on what you've learned. Pray the prayer you wrote to God and ask for help to live for Him today.

5. **Share:** Prayerfully reflect on who needs to hear the truths God has revealed to you. Write down their name, pray for them, and consider a time you could intentionally share what you're learning with them.

    Remember: God's Word is not just for you, but for others also. Share with others what you learned and tell them how you obeyed and applied the Scripture to your life. They might be able to hold you accountable and figure out ways to help you obey God's Word. Often, you will find God's Spirit has already been talking to them about the same concepts or truths, and they will be thrilled you are being used by God in this process.

To start a dialogue with others about what God is showing you in your reading, you might use the phrase, *"As I was reading the Bible today, I sensed God showed me something, and I thought about sharing it with you,"* or, *"I was wondering what you might think about what I am processing,"* and wait for a response. If the Holy Spirit is working in their heart, they will ask to hear more. Share your faith with those who engage in conversation.

An Example of SOAPS

Let's give a short example of how your notes might look using SOAPS from a short passage of Scripture:

Pray and then read this passage multiple times:

"'Therefore whoever hears these sayings of Mine, and does them, I will liken him to a wise man who built his house on the rock: and the rain descended, the floods came, and the winds blew and beat on that house; and it did not fall, for it was founded on the rock. But everyone who hears these sayings of Mine, and does not do them, will be like a foolish man who built his house on the sand: and the rain descended, the floods came, and the winds blew and beat on that house; and it fell. And great was its fall.' And so it was, when Jesus had ended these sayings, that the people were astonished at

His teaching, for He taught them as one having authority, and not as the scribes (Matthew 7:24-27).

1. **Scripture**
   - Everyone who hears these sayings and does them vs. those who hear and do not do them.
   - The people were astonished at His teaching.

2. **Observation**
   - The wise person's house will stand, and the foolish person's house will probably fall when the storms of life come. And the storms will come. I want to be "founded on the rock."
   - Jesus' teaching was very different from the average teachers. What does it mean to have "authority" when teaching?
   - Everyone heard the same message from Jesus; the difference was not in hearing, but in those who put into action what they heard. They were obedient.
   - Are there any areas in which I am not listening and being obedient to Jesus?

3. **Application**
   - What areas of my life today might be inconsistent with what Scripture teaches? Jesus, I feel like I am struggling with worry, and I know you want me to cast all of my cares on You. Help me do that today.
   - I want to be someone who has a level of spiritual authority. God, help me know Your Word and be sensitive to the Spirit so that I share only the truth of who You are and what You desire in a way that impacts others.

4. **Pray**
   - After a few minutes of prayer and asking Jesus what He wants from me, I wrote the following:

Lord Jesus, I want to say "yes" to anything you ask of me and be obedient in every area of my life today. As I read Your words and am trying to be sensitive to Your Spirit, please let me have ears to hear, a heart to respond, and Your strength to be able to accomplish all that You would ask me to do. May I build my life upon You and Your truth! Amen.

5. **Share**
   - I sensed during my prayer to share with these two people specifically this week:

     Jesus, help me to share with JoAnne this week, as I know she is going through some storms in her life and she is trying to find some direction. Help her have ears to hear. Also, help me to share with Timmy, as he is wanting to follow You, but he is not being obedient to what you say. Help me share that the difference between the wise and foolish is obedience to Jesus.

SOAPS is **that** simple and practical. It can be done in ten minutes, or you could spend hours using this tool over many passages. The key is to spend time with Jesus regularly, listening to His Spirit and His Word. By doing this, we grow in our understanding of Him, apply what we learn to our lives, and then share with others what we are learning. This will help us continually feed ourselves and mature as a disciple who can then help make more disciples. Now let's take some time to practice using this tool.

Model & Practice: Personal Bible Study

There are several passages of Scripture for you to practice this method of personal Bible study below. Your trainer will choose one passage and model how to effectively use this method. After your trainer models the method, practice together using the template on the next page.

Suggested Passages to Practice:
The Shepherd and His Sheep *(John 10:22-30)*
Abiding in Christ *(John 15:1-9)*
The Prodigal Son *(Luke 15:11-24)*
Prayer *(Matthew 6:5-15)*
Fellowship *(Acts 2:41-47)*
Being a Witness *(Acts 1:3-9)*
The Greatest Commandment *(Mark 12:28-34)*
Parable of the Soils *(Matthew 13:3-8, 18-23)*
Parable of the Talents *(Matthew 25:14-30)*
Parable of the Persistent Widow *(Luke 18:2-8)*
The Cost of Discipleship *(Luke 14:25-33)*
Samaritan Woman at the Well *(John 4:7-45)*
Boldness in the Face of Persecution *(Acts 4:23-31)*

Personal Bible Study Template

SOAPS

Scripture

Observation

Application

Pray

Share

Action Steps for this chapter:

- Write new "I will" statements in your chapter journal. What will you do today and this week in response to God's voice?

- Study the Bible using the SOAPS Bible study method at least one time this week in your devotional time. Be prepared to share what you have learned and with whom you shared it at the next training. Make sure to follow through on your "I will" statements.

- Follow up with those you have been sharing with. Encourage anyone you lead to Christ to study Scripture with the SOAPS study method you learned in this chapter.

- Continue sharing your story and God's story with at least two to three people this week. **Be ready to report back on what happened.**

Chapter Journal

I will: _____

_____

_____

I will: _____

_____

_____

I will: _____

_____

_____

I will: _____

_____

_____

Notes:

_____

_____

_____

_____

_____

Chapter 7 Trainer's Guide
A Daily Relationship with God

Training Goal (Heartbeat): Show every disciple maker how to create a daily routine of spending time in God's Word, hearing His voice, and immediately obeying what He spoke.

Expected Outcome (Skill/Habit): Every disciple maker will set aside time every day to spend with God that includes the reading of His Word, prayer, and responding in obedience.

 Look Back

Give everyone a chance to share, hear from others, and be held accountable. Focus on encouragement, celebration, and following through with assignments.

- **Obedience:** Have <u>everyone</u> report back on how they shared their story, God's story, and followed through with their "I will" statements since the last training. (This can be done as a large group or in smaller groups.) It is important not to move forward with Chapter 7 until everyone has put into practice what they learned about the SOAPS study method. **Remember: Be intentional to lovingly hold those you train accountable.**
  - o Did you study the Bible using the SOAPS study method?
  - o How many days did you use the SOAPS method during your daily devotional time?
  - o How did the conversations go with those whom the Holy Spirit told you to share?
- **Review:** Go over the expected outcome and key principle from Chapter 6. Summarize the key points learned from the previous training.
- **Remind:** Training is for trainers. Did you train anyone in how to pray?

Before Looking Up, have at least two people practice sharing their story or God's story in front of the group.

# Look Up

This chapter introduces the importance of spending time alone with God in order to have a personal relationship with Him. Be sure to focus on these key concepts:

- Train in a way that every disciple maker is able to pray and have personal devotions with God on a daily basis.
- Emphasize the importance of setting aside a specific time daily to talk with God and spend time in His Word. As disciples, we must hear His voice and be ready to immediately obey what He calls you to do.
- **Remember to highlight the expected outcome and key principle!** Encourage memorization of key Scripture verses.
- **Hearing from God:** Allow for a time of silent prayer and reflection, specifically looking for what each person should do in response to God speaking to their heart.

Model & Practice: Model how they do their own daily devotions. Encourage those you disciple to practice this week.

Look Forward

Before reviewing the action steps for the chapter, pause and prayerfully discuss the following questions:

- How is God speaking to your heart today?
- How is God calling you to greater obedience?
- What will you do today and this week in response to God's voice?

Action Steps for this chapter:

- Write new "I will" statements in your chapter journal.
- Are you willing to commit to a daily devotion? **Identify who will encourage and hold you accountable to your commitment.** Encourage and challenge those you disciple to set a specific time and place when they will have a daily devotion. Show them how and hold them accountable to it!
- Remember to pray daily for God to lead you to pre-Christians. Also, continue sharing your story and God's story with more people this week. **Be prepared to report the results of your sharing with your trainer!**

Chapter 7
A Daily Relationship with God

Expected Outcome: Every disciple maker will set aside time every day to spend with God that includes the reading of His Word, prayer, and responding in obedience.

In the last two chapters, you learned how to spend time with God on a regular basis through Scripture reading and prayer. When you practice those skills daily, it is often referred to as a "daily devotion." When you make a daily devotion an ongoing habit in your life, you will find that your relationship with God can grow tremendously. We need to embrace this reality: **The God of the universe wants to spend time alone with you, every day!** A daily devotion is one of the best ways to enjoy that relationship with our Creator.

All throughout the Gospels, Jesus made a habit of going away by Himself to spend time with God. *"Now in the morning, having risen a long while before daylight, He went out and departed to a solitary place; and there He prayed"* (Mark 1:35; See also: Luke 5:16; Matthew 14:23; Luke 22:39-44). If Jesus made an effort to regularly pray and spend time with His Father, how much more do we need it today?

Two Simple Components to a Devotional Life
1. Talk with and listen to God through prayer (based on what you learned in Chapter 5).
2. Let God speak to you by reading and reflecting on the Bible and listening to the Holy Spirit (using SOAPS in Chapter 6 and practicing Chapter 1).

The Purpose of Our Devotional Life
1. **To worship God**: To honor and enjoy Him!
2. **To grow in our relationship with God:** We connect with Him and are able to share our joys and concerns as we draw closer to Him.
3. **To be led by God**: To obey His will and plans for our lives as we point others towards Him.

Group Discussion: Read *Psalm 42:1* and *Psalm 119:147-148* together. Discuss how the writer regarded God and how he felt about spending time with God when he wrote these psalms. Describe his attitude and honestly assess your own feelings and desires for meditating on God and His Word.

Tools for Your Daily Devotions

Bible: Read or listen to the Scriptures every day, and then write down or share with someone what you learned from the reading. Reflect on what you read throughout the day. Reading God's Word is so powerful in our lives that it answers some of life's greatest questions like: Where do I come from? Why do I exist? How should I live? What happens when I die?

Journal/Notes: During your devotional time, you will need to be able to write down what you sense God is saying to you and the names and needs of those you are praying for. It may be beneficial to have a second pad of paper to write down things that come to your mind that interrupt your time with God. During your time of prayer, you may remember you have to mow the grass, get milk, or call a friend. Write down the things that are distracting you on the second pad of paper. This allows you to clear your mind from interruptions and distractions, so you can focus on God. When you are finished with your devotions, you can shift focus to your to-do list.

Time & Place: Choose a time and place where you can consistently meet with God without being disturbed. Consider putting your phone on silent or (if possible) in another room. Creating an environment where you can draw near to God will make that time all the more fruitful.

Plan: Read the Bible with intentionality, meditate, take notes, pray, and obey. It is helpful to use a Bible reading plan to organize your reading. You can download an app with various reading plan options at www.youversion.com.

Group Discussion: What other tools do you use that help you have a more effective daily time with God? Share how you use them and why they are helpful for your devotional time. Do you have a time and place that is already working for you? Why did you choose that place and time?

How to Meditate on God's Word

Meditating on God's Word is intentionally letting its truths permeate the depths of your heart. It's not just about knowing God's truth; it's about taking the time to reflect on, process, and absorb its truths into the core of who you are. God's Word is living and active. This is why the same passage and the same questions will speak to our heart differently every time.

As you read a passage each day, seek to ask yourself good questions about how these truths can transform your life like we practiced in the SOAPS method:

- What captured your attention in this passage?
- What did you like about this passage?
- Did anything bother you? Why?
- What did you learn about God?
- What did you learn about people?
- Is there an example to follow?
- Is there a command to obey?
- Is there an action to avoid?
- Is there a promise to claim?
- With whom should you share this truth?

*Important Note: There may not be an answer to each question in every passage. Focus on the answers that apply.

Developing Your Devotional Life

It is essential for your growth as a follower of Jesus that you be faithful in keeping your daily devotions. Like any other important meeting you have during the day, put it in your calendar or set a reminder on your phone. Choose a regular time and place to which you can commit. **Make your time with God a daily priority.**

How often you choose to meet with God will be the most important decision in your walk with God. If you neglect it, you will lose the power to be used by God and fulfill the mission for which He created you. The one similarity that every great man or woman of God throughout history have in common was that they spent significant time alone with God daily.

It is your decision how often you meet with God. Setting aside daily time with God will be a catalyst to spiritual growth and the deepening of your relationship with Him.

While Jesus was on this earth, He said, *"Seek first the kingdom of God and His righteousness" (Matthew 6:33).* Of all the things you could encounter in this world, there is nothing more important than encountering God on a consistent basis. **If you are too busy to spend time with God, you are too busy! Your priorities need to be reorganized!**

One of God's desires is for you to have fellowship with Him and to know Him. Your goal should be to praise and worship God by meeting Him on a consistent basis through reading His Word and by talking to Him in prayer.

 Key Principle: The main purpose of daily devotions is to know and worship God and respond in obedience to His Word and Spirit.

Model & Practice: Daily Devotions

Your trainer will now take time to model exactly how they do their own daily devotions with prayer and the SOAPS Bible study method, answering any questions you may have so that you can also practice it in your own life.

Group Discussion: Gather in groups of two or three and discuss how you do your daily devotions and any changes/additions that need to be made based on this chapter.

Action Steps for this chapter:
- Write new "I will" statements in your chapter journal. What specific thing can you do in response to hearing God's voice today and this week?
- Are you willing to commit to a daily devotion? **Identify who will encourage and hold you accountable to your commitment.** Encourage and challenge those you disciple to set a specific time and place when they will have a daily devotion. Show them how and hold them accountable to it!

Time:

Place:

- Remember to pray daily for God to lead you to pre-Christians. Also, continue sharing your story and God's story with more people this week. **Be prepared to report the results of your sharing with your trainer!**

Chapter Journal

I will: _____

_____

_____

I will: _____

_____

_____

I will: _____

_____

_____

I will: _____

_____

_____

Notes:

_____

_____

_____

_____

_____

Additional study for this chapter:

As you grow in your prayer and devotional life, it is important to recognize that the Christian life is not only about your personal relationship with God, but about God's plan to save all people. **Being a follower of Jesus involves a lifelong commitment to help others follow Jesus.**

- Read *Psalm 139:13-16* and *Acts 17:24-28.* What theme do you see when you read these verses?

- We must understand that God has uniquely designed, gifted, and placed us in specific networks and relationships so that others may also know Him. Who are you helping to follow Jesus?

You are not in your family, neighborhood, school, or workplace by mistake. God has uniquely designed you and has placed you exactly where you should be. Are you being obedient? Are you walking in the Spirit? If you don't share Christ with them, who will?

Chapter 8 Trainer's Guide
Discovery Bible Study

Training Goal (Heartbeat): Explain the value of training the next generation by equipping every disciple maker to confidently lead a Discovery Bible Study.

Expected Outcome (Skill/Habit): Every disciple maker will gather a group of new believers or "pre-Christians" to lead them through a Discovery Bible Study so they can begin to read God's Word, hear His voice, and respond in obedience.

 ## Look Back

Give everyone a chance to share, hear from others, and be held accountable. Focus on encouragement, celebration, and following through with assignments.

- **Obedience:** Have <u>everyone</u> report back on how they shared their story, God's story, and followed through with their "I will" statements since the last training. (This can be done as a large group or in smaller groups.) Do not move forward with Chapter 8 until everyone has put into practice what they learned about daily devotions.
- **Review:** Go over the expected outcome and key principle from Chapter 7. Ask how it went practicing a daily devotion and get feedback and insight.
- **Remind:** All training is for trainers. You need to be training others what you have learned. Did you train anyone how to pray?

Before Looking Up, have at least two people practice sharing their story or God's story in front of the group.

 ## Look Up

This chapter introduces the concept of a group Bible study method called Discovery Bible Study. The way you model the study will be how they reproduce it. Ensure you feel confident in leading a group prior to the training. As you train those you are discipling through this chapter, be sure to focus on these key concepts:

- Train in a way that every disciple maker is able to reproduce the model you are training.
- **Remember to highlight the expected outcome and key principle!**
- **Hearing from God:** At the end of this chapter, allow for a time of silent prayer and reflection, specifically looking for what each person should do in response to God speaking to their heart.

Model & Practice: Model how to lead a Group Discovery Bible Study. Encourage those you disciple to practice leading one this week.

 # Look Forward

Before reviewing the action steps for the chapter, pause and prayerfully discuss the following questions:
- How is God speaking to your heart today?
- How is God calling you to greater obedience?
- What will you do today and this week in response to God's voice?

Action Steps for this chapter:
- Write new "I will" statements in your chapter journal. What will you do today and this week in response to God's voice?
- Prayerfully consider starting a Discovery Bible Study with those you are already discipling. Or, consider starting a study that will reach your friends, family, coworkers and/or those with whom you have been praying to share your story and God's story.
- If you start a Discovery Bible Study, invite anyone with whom you share your story or God's story (even if you just met them) to join your group or someone else's group from your Training Center to which they might be willing to go.
- Consider talking with someone else in your Training Center about starting a group together for synergy and mutual support and then multiplying later as the group grows.

Chapter 8
Discovery Bible Study

Expected Outcome: Every disciple maker will gather a group of new believers or "pre-Christians" to lead them through a Discovery Bible Study so they can begin to read God's Word, hear His voice, and respond in obedience.

Learning how to discover the Bible as a group is a critical part of a long-term plan for multiplying disciples and churches. In Chapter 6, we introduced SOAPS as a way to do personal Bible study. This chapter introduces a practical Bible study method that builds on what you learned from SOAPS and applies to groups studying Scripture together. This method has been used in countries all over the world, in a variety of cultures and contexts. It is highly effective and easy for anyone to do.

One of the benefits of this method of study is that it can be done with people who may not have a relationship with Jesus or any prior biblical knowledge or background. It can also be practiced by fully devoted, mature believers. The power comes from reading Scripture in community, asking good questions, and allowing the best teacher, the Holy Spirit, to challenge and encourage us. **Remember,** *"The word of God is living and powerful, and sharper than any two-edged sword, piercing even to the division of soul and spirit, and of joints and marrow, and is a discerner of the thoughts and intents of the heart" (Hebrews 4:12).*

How to Do Group Discovery Bible Study

As you meet with a group of those you are discipling or who have some spiritual interest, it is good to follow the normal practice we have been using of looking back, looking up, and looking forward.

As you begin by looking back, have everyone share one thing they are **thankful** for and one thing that is causing **anxiety or**

fear in their life. Point out to the group that one aspect of prayer is telling God the things we are thankful for and talking with Him about what worries or stresses us out. As everyone shares, pray for one another.

The Holy Spirit

Right after you pray, ask the group to share what God said to them in their personal time (devotions) with Him since your last meeting. Asking this question at the beginning of every meeting encourages group members to have a personal time with God.

Giving them an opportunity to share allows room for the Holy Spirit to take the group study in a completely different direction than you planned. Be sensitive to the group and make sure everyone has time to share what God is showing them.

After this time, ask the group to share how they have done on their "I will" statements since the last gathering. This will encourage and hold each other accountable to ensure we are being obedient to what we are learning and hearing from God.

Scripture

After everyone has a chance to share, choose a passage of Scripture and have someone read it aloud while everyone follows along in their Bibles (or listens carefully, for those without Bibles or who are illiterate). When they are done, have someone else read the same passage aloud again. This time have everyone just listen to the passage as the person reads. When they are done, ask for a volunteer to retell the passage in their own words. When they finish, ask the group to fill in any points they feel were left out.

Reading, listening, and retelling Scripture is very important. It allows everyone time to think about the passage and ask the Holy Spirit to speak to them through His Word. Retelling the passage allows them to think through how they can share

116

this passage with someone outside the group. Allowing the group to add to the retelling encourages everyone to think about the main points in the passage. Even though going through the passage multiple times may seem repetitive and time consuming, the process helps develop healthy disciples and retain what you are learning.

Discovery Study
After your group retells the Scripture, you can study the passage. Your discussion should be filled with questions that aid your discussion and get to the heart of the passage. Questions facilitate the discovery process and allow your group to interact with Scripture and grow spiritually. You should use many of the same questions you use for your personal devotional time as you interact with Scripture. This allows our interaction with Scripture to be easily reproducible as we train other disciples. Below are the questions:
- What did you like about this passage?
- Did anything concern you? Why?
- What does this passage teach us about God?
- What does this passage teach us about people?
- Is there an example to follow?
- Is there a command to obey or action to take?
- Is there a sin to avoid?
- Is there a promise to claim?
- With whom should you share this truth?

Keep discussion focused on Scripture. If you or someone else in your group is knowledgeable of the Bible, it may be hard to avoid introducing outside materials into the study. The leader needs to work hard to limit the sharing of popular opinions or extra-biblical materials. These opinions and materials do not facilitate interaction with Scripture. **Do your best to keep discussion focused on the Scripture and guided by the Holy Spirit.**

117

Commitment

Knowledge of God's Word must lead to obedience and sharing with others. This next step begins with a statement and a question:

"<u>Since we believe God's Word is true, **what** must we change in our lives to obey God?</u>"

Everyone in the group should answer this question before finishing. If they already obey this Scripture, have them share how they obey it and how they have trained others also. Ask if there is anything they need to do to increase their obedience to God's Word in this area of their life. Keep this part of your time <u>focused on specific action steps</u>.

After everyone shares how they are going to obey Scripture, have them identify someone who needs to hear what God said to the group. Encourage them to share what they learned with that person. Before you finish, ask the group to identify people they know who are in need. Ask the group to identify ways to meet those needs in the next week. Finally, close with prayer.

 Key Principle: By participating in a Discovery Bible Study, we can grow in our relationship with God and be mutually encouraged by others.

Summary of Group Discovery Bible Study

 Looking Back

- **Opening prayer:** Begin by having the group share one thing they are thankful for and one challenge or fear they are facing. Allow for a time of group prayer.
- **What did God say:** Ask each person to share what they sense God has taught them through His Word since the last meeting.
- **What did I do:** Ask each person to share how they have been obedient to God since the previous meeting. Also, ask about their "I will" statements.

 Looking Up

- **Read:** Read the portion of Scripture aloud while people follow along in their Bibles.
- **Re-read:** Have someone else read the same passage aloud while the group listens.
- **Share in your own words:** Have someone else in the group retell the passage in their own words. Allow the group to add to the retelling, if necessary.
- **Discovery questions:** Use discovery questions to encourage the group to interact with the passage.
- **Pray:** Have everyone take two minutes to pray and ask, "What will I do in response to what I have learned from Scripture and God's Spirit today?"

 Looking Forward

- **Obey God's Word: Have each person write down their "I will" statement and then share with the group what they are going to do to obey the passage over the next week.**
- **Action plan:** Have the group identify people they will share the passage with during the next week and write down their names. Have the group identify people in need and commit to meeting those needs.
- **Commitment and closing prayer**

Some Common Questions about Discovery Bible Study:

What about those who cannot read?

The discovery process for those who cannot read is similar to the group process outlined above, just listening instead of reading. Allowing the group to retell the passage is even more important in oral settings because repetition helps them remember the passage.

Can non-Christians participate in the Group Discovery Bible Study process?

Yes, everyone has the opportunity to hear God's voice and respond in obedience. For non-Christians specifically, try these sorts of questions:

- "If this story is true, how does that change how we act?"
- "What questions do you have about this story?"
- "Do you know anyone who needs to hear this story?"
- "Does anyone want to accept Christ?"

Encourage them to share the story with anyone they name.

Ask: "Is there anyone we know who needs help (physical, emotional, financial, practical)? What can we do to help them?"

Have the group decide what needs to be done and together commit to doing it before the next meeting.

Some Guidelines for Leading a Discovery Bible Study:

1. Let the Bible speak for itself and don't feel the need to have an answer for every question that is asked. Keep pointing back to Scripture and ask, "What does the Scripture say?" Give space for processing and for the Holy Spirit to speak.
2. If someone asks an important question but you do not have an answer, simply say, "That's a good question, but I don't know how to answer it. Let me study and maybe talk

with some friends, and we can follow up with that next week."

3. If your group grows larger, break into groups at the beginning and/or the end as you share what God has been doing in your life or as you share your "I will" statements. Come back together for the Bible study portion to ensure that everyone has time to share.

Model & Practice: Leading A Discovery Bible Study

Your trainer will now model how to use the Discovery Bible Study Method using the sample lesson from Genesis below. Make sure you ask questions if you need clarity on anything.

Action Steps for the chapter:

• Write new "I will" statements in your chapter journal. What will you do today and this week in response to God's voice?

• Prayerfully consider starting a Discovery Bible Study with others you are already discipling. Or, consider starting a study that will reach your friends, family, coworkers, and/or any of those for whom you have been praying to share your story and God's story.

• If you start a Discovery Bible Study, invite anyone with whom you share your story or God's story (even if you just met them) to join your group or someone else's group from your Training Center to which they might be willing to go.

• Consider talking with someone else in your Training Center about starting a group together for synergy and mutual support and then multiplying later as the group grows.

Discovery Bible Study Sample Lesson
Genesis 1:1-25

 <u>Look Back</u>

- **Opening prayer:**
  - What are you thankful for today?
  - What sort of problems are you facing?
  - Is there any way this group can help you? Pray.
- **What did God say?**
- **What did I do?**

 <u>Look Up</u>

- **Read: Genesis 1:1-25**
- **Re-read:**
  - Have someone else read the same passage aloud while the group listens.
- **Share in your own words:**
  - Have someone else in the group retell the passage in their own words. Allow the group to add to the retelling, if necessary.
- **Discovery questions:**
  - Use discovery questions to encourage the group to interact with the passage.
    - What did you like about this passage?
    - Did anything concern you? Why?
    - What does this passage teach us about God?
    - What does this passage teach us about people?
    - Is there an example to follow?
    - Is there a command to obey or action to take?
    - Is there a sin to avoid?
    - Is there a promise to claim?
    - With whom should you share this truth?
  - Ask questions until they discover the basic idea: There is a God who created the world.
  - After the group has discovered truths from God's

Word, help them identify what difference this makes in their lives.

- **Pray:**
  - Have everyone take two minutes to pray, and ask, "What will I do in response to what I have learned from Scripture and God's Spirit today?"

 Look Forward

- **Obey God's Word:**
  - Have each person share what they are going to do to obey the passage over the next week.
  - Ask questions to help individuals and groups tell how their lives can change if they live like the passage is true. Help them move from a general statement to a specific statement.
    - If this passage is true, how does this passage change how we see God?
    - If this passage is true, how does this passage change how we treat others?
    - If this passage is true, how does this passage change how we live?
    - What other questions do you have about this passage?
- **Action plan:**
  - Do you know anyone with whom you can share this story?
  - Do you know anyone who needs help? What can this group do to help them?
- **Commitment and closing prayer**

Recommended Discovery Bible Study Lessons

The progression of these passages is designed to help you take lost people or new believers through the Bible with the purpose of laying a solid foundation to help you lead them to Christ.

1. God Creates *(Genesis 1:1-25)*

2. God Creates Man and Woman *(Genesis 2:4-24)*

3. Man and Woman Eat the Fruit *(Genesis 3:1-13)*

4. God's Curses *(Genesis 3:14-24)*

5. God Regrets His Creation *(Genesis 6:5-8)*

6. God Saves Noah and His Family *(Genesis 6:9-8:14)*

7. God's Covenant with Noah *(Genesis 8:15-9:17)*

8. God's Covenant with Abram *(Genesis 12:1-8; 15:1-6; 17:1-7)*

9. Abraham Gives His Son as an Offering *(Genesis 22:1-19)*

10. God Spares His People *(Exodus 12:1-28)*

11. The Commands of God *(Exodus 20:1-21)*

12. The Sin Offering *(Leviticus 4:1-35)*

13. God's Righteous Servant *(Isaiah 53)*

14. Jesus Is Born *(Luke 1:26-38; 2:1-20)*

15. Jesus Is Baptized *(Matthew 3; John 1:29-34)*

16. Jesus Is Tested *(Matthew 4:1-11)*

17. Jesus and the Religious Leader *(John 3:1-21)*

18. Jesus and the Samaritan Woman *(John 4:1-26, 39-42)*

19. Jesus and the Paralyzed Man *(Luke 5:17-26)*

20. Jesus Calms the Storm *(Mark 4:35-41)*

21. Jesus and the Man with Evil Spirits *(Mark 5:1-20)*

22. Jesus Raises a Man from the Dead *(John 11:1-44)*

23. Jesus Talks about His Betrayal and the Covenant *(Matthew 26:17-30)*

24. Jesus Is Betrayed and Faces Trial *(John 18:1-19:16)*

25. Jesus Is Crucified *(Luke 23:32-56)*

26. Jesus Is Resurrected *(Luke 24:1-35)*

27. Jesus Appears to the Disciples and Ascends to Heaven *(Luke 24:36-53)*

28. Enter into the Kingdom of God *(John 3:1-21)*

Chapter Journal

I will: _____

_____

_____

I will: _____

_____

_____

I will: _____

_____

_____

I will: _____

_____

_____

Notes:

_____

_____

_____

_____

_____

Chapter 9 Trainer's Guide
God Our Heavenly Father

Training Goal (Heartbeat): Help every disciple maker have a biblical understanding of God and how they can best respond to every situation in their life.

Expected Outcome (Skill/Habit): Every disciple maker will make decisions and choices informed by a biblical understanding of who God is and what He is like.

 ## Look Back

Give everyone a chance to share, hear from others, and be held accountable. Focus on encouragement, celebration, and following through with assignments.

- **Obedience:** Have <u>everyone</u> report back on how they shared their story, God's story, and followed through with what they said they would do since the last training. (This can be done as a large group or in smaller groups.) Do not move forward with Chapter 9 before putting into practice what was taught in the previous chapter. Did you get a chance to do a DBS with someone or with a group? If not, with whom has God put on your heart to start a DBS?
- **Review:** Go over the expected outcome and key principle from Chapter 8. Summarize the key points learned from the previous training.
- **Remind:** All training is for trainers. Are they training others with what they are learning?

Before Looking Up, have at least two people practice sharing their story or God's story in front of the group.

 ## Look Up

This chapter highlights how God, our Heavenly Father, reveals His unconditional love towards His children. He loves, protects, provides for, and disciplines His children. As you train those you are discipling through this chapter, be sure to focus on these key concepts:

- Train in a way that every disciple understands the blessings that come with being unconditionally loved by God, our all-powerful, all-knowing Heavenly Father who is always with us.
- **Remember to highlight the expected outcome and key principle!**
- Encourage memorization of key Scripture verses.
- **Hearing from God:** At the end of this chapter, allow for a time of silent prayer and reflection specifically looking for what each person should do in response to God speaking to their heart.

Group Discussion: Which of these four points is most meaningful to you and why? Which of these is most difficult to embrace? Explain why and share with the group.

Model & Practice: Take time to explain how a biblical understanding of who God is and His attributes affect how the disciple maker will respond to different situations and circumstances in life.

 ## Look Forward

Before reviewing the action steps for the chapter, pause and prayerfully discuss the following questions:
- How is God speaking to your heart today?
- How is God calling you to greater obedience?
- What will you do today and this week in response to God's voice?

Action Steps for this chapter:
- Write new "I will" statements in your chapter journal. What will you do today and this week in response to God's voice?
- Complete the additional study for this chapter on God and His attributes.
- Share the truths you learn about God and His love in the additional study with someone who needs to hear them.
- **Memorize** *John 3:16* or *Titus 3:4-5.*
- Continue sharing your story and God's story with those on your list. Be ready to report back on what happened.

Chapter 9
God Our Heavenly Father

Expected Outcome: Every disciple maker will make decisions and choices informed by a biblical understanding of who God is and what He is like.

Our understanding of who God is and what He is like directly impacts what we think it means to be His disciple. If you have a poor perception of God, it will reflect in every area of your life. In *The Knowledge of the Holy*, A.W. Tozer writes,

> *What comes into our minds when we think about God is the most important thing about us ... The most essential aspect of any man is not what he may say or do, but what his deep heart conceives God to be like.*

The goal of this chapter is to challenge you to wrestle with what you actually believe about who God is and what He is like. A secondary goal is to create an insatiable thirst within you to pursue knowing God like never before. By the end of this chapter, we trust the first thing that comes to your mind when you think about God will be informed by what the Bible says about Him and His great love for you, evidenced in the Gospel.

God is indescribable and beyond our comprehension. There is no more worthwhile endeavor than to pursue growing in our understanding and friendship with Him. Read some of the ways God can be described on the following pages.

All-Powerful

"In the beginning God created the heavens and the earth. Then God said, 'Let there be light'; and there was light. Then God said, 'Let there be a firmament in the midst of the waters, and let it divide the waters from the waters.' Then God said, 'Let the waters under the heavens be gathered together into one place, and let the dry land appear'; and it was so" (Genesis 1:1, 3, 6, 9).

God is the all-powerful Creator of the universe. The vastness of our universe, its incredible complexity and its creative design, is God's power on display. God spoke the universe into existence from nothingness.

Everything is perfectly designed and put in its precise place by God. The earth is 93 million miles from the sun, which is the exact distance needed to sustain life. No other planet in our solar system has any observable evidence of life or the environmental conditions needed to produce life. The complexity and intelligent design of the human body is incredible. Our heart beats, our lungs breathe, and our blood flows, independent of our efforts. When we become sick or break a bone, our bodies begin to heal themselves with cells specifically designed to fight viruses and make repairs. Imagine if a car that was leaking oil could patch itself without the help of a mechanic; that is how the human body functions!

The most amazing part about this all-powerful and infinite God is that He loves us. He doesn't lord His power over us but used it to raise Jesus from the dead. He did this so that we could have a relationship with Him. The same power that God used to raise Jesus from the dead was entrusted to Jesus' disciples and fills us when we are reconciled to God through faith in Jesus Christ.

Always Present

"Where can I go from Your Spirit? Or where can I flee from Your presence? If I ascend into heaven, You are there; If I make my bed in hell, behold, You are there. If I take the wings of the morning, And dwell in the uttermost parts of the sea, Even there your hand shall lead me, and Your right hand shall hold me" (Psalm 139:7-10).

God is present everywhere at once. There isn't a place on earth you can go to escape His presence. As a disciple of Jesus, the more we become aware that God's presence is always with us wherever we go, the more we will begin to live like Jesus.

Realizing that God is with you dramatically affects your everyday decisions in profound ways. Since God is always with us, we can have courage when we face seemingly impossible situations or circumstances. We can exercise self-control in the midst of temptation because He sees us and is with us. We can have patience and peace even when chaos is all around us because we know that God is with us in the midst of our suffering.

Remember what Moses said to God before Israel entered the land God had promised to Abraham, Isaac, and Jacob: *"If Your Presence does not go with us, do not bring us up from here"* (Exodus 33:15). It is important that we realize that God's presence is essential for the effectiveness of the church and our ability to make disciples. Begin fostering your awareness of God's presence moment by moment by *"pray[ing] without ceasing"* (1 Thessalonians 5:17). Talk to Him and listen to Him because He's always near. Living every moment with the knowledge that you are in God's presence will give you a new perspective about your life and its purpose.

All-Knowing

"O LORD, You have searched me and known me. You know my sitting down and my rising up; You understand my thought afar off. You comprehend my path and my lying down, And are acquainted with all my ways. For there is not a word on my tongue, But behold, O LORD, You know it altogether" (Psalm 139:1-4).

God knows everything, and there isn't anything past, present, or future that God isn't aware of. He knows everything about us, everything we say, every thought we think, and every emotion we feel.

God not only knows everything about us, He even knows the future! Nearly one-third of Scripture is dedicated to prophecy. These prophecies demonstrate that God's Word is true and that He is all-knowing. When we see prophecies fulfilled, it's a confirmation that His promises are true and that He can be trusted.

God is the Creator and designer of the universe and He made humanity in His image. Doesn't it make sense that He knows what is best for us? In His grace and mercy towards us, God gave us His Word to guide and show us how to live this life to the fullest. While His ways are often more difficult to obey in the moment, they prove far better in the long run. What we desire for ourselves is often at odds with what God wants, and these sinful inclinations cause far more destruction than good (lies instead of integrity, lust/sexual sin instead of purity, greed instead of generosity, anxiety instead of trust).

Even though God designed us and knows what is best for us, we often choose to go our own way instead of obeying God's voice. In our selfishness and pride, we are essentially saying "God, I know better than you. My ways are higher than yours."

 Group Discussion: Take time to ask God what areas of your life you need to surrender to Him. Discuss the ways you need to realign your life with His ways.

All-Loving

"For God so loved the world that he gave His only begotten Son, that whoever believes in Him should not perish but have everlasting life" (John 3:16).

"But God demonstrates His own love toward us, in that while we were still sinners, Christ died for us" (Romans 5:8).

Imagine an all-powerful, all-knowing, ever present God who was not loving. This is the type of god that most nations and cultures throughout history have "worshiped." In the nations surrounding Israel during the time of the Bible, the gods were perceived as mysterious, distant, and frightening. In many nations in the world today, they still envision a vengeful, controlling, scary, or non-caring god. It is often unclear to many people what they need to do in order to earn the favor and acceptance of these gods. This is what sets the God of the Bible apart from every other god that people worshiped: His love for us and the world, and His desire to be known by us.

God's love for us is astounding and defies all reason. Consider just how irrational God's love is for us: Even though we were enemies of God, He loved us enough to send His son to take the punishment we deserved because we rebelled against Him. He did this so that we could have a relationship with Him and no longer be separated from His presence. As we reflect on His amazing love and grace, it compels us to live our lives as a living sacrifice for Him *(Romans 12:1-2).*

The best way to describe God's love for us is to see Him as our good and perfect "Father." In the Parable of the Prodigal Son, Jesus describes the relationship between a father and two sons that demonstrates God's love for us despite our rejection of Him.

133

Group Discussion: Read *Luke 15:11-32*. Discuss the similarities between this father and God, our Heavenly Father. In the table below, list the qualities you see in the father from the parable and consider what they teach us about our Heavenly Father.

Qualities of the Father	Teachings about the Heavenly Father

After reading and discussing the passage, reflect on this question: **In what ways has God revealed His love to you?**

Jesus teaches us to view God as our Heavenly Father. When Jesus taught His disciples to pray, He started with *"Our Father in heaven."* The Bible also describes God as our Father. Just like a good father, He loves, protects, provides for, and disciplines His children.

 Key Principle: God is your Heavenly Father and loves you unconditionally.

1. **The Heavenly Father's Love**

 Group Discussion: Read through the passages below and discuss how God loves you and why God saved you.

134

"But when the kindness and the love of God our Savior toward man appeared, not by works of righteousness which we have done, but according to His mercy He saved us, through the washing of regeneration and renewing of the Holy Spirit" (Titus 3:4-5).

"But God, who is rich in mercy, because of His great love with which He loved us, even when we were dead in trespasses, made us alive together with Christ" (Ephesians 2:4-5).

"The LORD has appeared of old to me, saying: 'Yes, I have loved you with an everlasting love; Therefore with lovingkindness I have drawn you" (Jeremiah 31:3).

2. The Heavenly Father's Protection

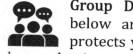 **Group Discussion:** Read through the passages below and consider how the Heavenly Father protects you. As you discuss these passages, write down what impacts you most.

"But the Lord is faithful, who will establish you and guard you from the evil one" (2 Thessalonians 3:3).

"The angel of the LORD encamps all around those who fear Him, And delivers them" (Psalm 34:7).

"And when the servant of the man of God arose early and went out, there was an army, surrounding the city with horses and chariots. And his servant said to him, 'Alas, my master! What shall we do?' So, he answered, 'Do not fear, for those who are with us are more than those who are with them.' And Elisha prayed, and said, 'LORD, I pray, open his eyes that he may see.' Then the LORD opened the eyes of the young man, and he saw. And behold, the mountain was full of horses and chariots of fire all around Elisha. So when the Syrians came down to him, Elisha prayed to the LORD, and said, 'Strike this people, I pray, with blindness.' And He struck them with blindness according to the word of Elisha" (2 Kings 6:15-18).

"No temptation has overtaken you except such as is common to man; but God is faithful, who will not allow you to be tempted beyond what you are able, but with the temptation will also make the way of escape, that you may be able to bear it" *(1 Corinthians 10:13).*

What impacted you most from these passages?

3. The Heavenly Father's Provision

 Group Discussion: Read through the passages below and discuss how the Heavenly Father provides.

"And my God shall supply all your need according to His riches in glory by Christ Jesus" *(Philippians 4:19).*

"Therefore do not worry, saying, 'What shall we eat?' or 'What shall we drink?' or 'What shall we wear?' For after all these things the Gentiles seek. For your heavenly Father knows that you need all these things. But seek first the kingdom of God and His righteousness, and all these things shall be added to you" *(Matthew 6:31-33).*

"He who did not spare His own Son, but delivered Him up for us all, how shall He not with Him also freely give us all things?" *(Romans 8:32)*

How do these verses of God's provision help you understand that you can trust Him in the midst of difficulty or hardship?

4. The Heavenly Father's Discipline

A Biblical Definition of Discipline

In the New Testament, **discipline** carries the idea of *instruction* and *training*. The primary motivation and goal of discipline was to teach and encourage self-control. Consider the example of raising a child. When you discipline a child, you are training them to exercise self-control over their actions and instructing them in the way they ought to live. In the same way that parents use discipline to ensure their children do not hurt themselves or others, so God disciplines His children in His Word and through His Spirit. God disciplines out of His love for us and a desire to encourage us to pursue His righteousness. God desires to help the individual become all that He designed them to be.

"'For whom the LORD loves He chastens, And scourges every son whom He recieves.' If you endure chastening, God deals with you as with sons; for what son is there whom a father does not chasten?" (Hebrews 12:6–7)

"All Scripture is given by inspiration of God, and is profitable for doctrine, for reproof, for correction, for instruction in righteousness" (2 Timothy 3:16).

 Group Discussion: Which aspect of God from above or the list below is most meaningful to you and why? Which is most difficult for you to embrace or accept? Explain why and share with the group.

- He is all-knowing, and He understands what is best.
- He is always present.
- He is all-powerful.
- He loves us and is kind.
- He protects us.
- He provides for our needs.
- He disciplines us because He loves us.
- Knowing His will, character, and nature
- Something else?

Model & Practice: God's Identity Empowers Our Actions

 Group Discussion: How does your understanding of who God is and His attributes affect how you respond to the following situations?

Your trainer will lead you through these questions below. Knowing who God is and what He is like can empower you to live a transformed life. Consider writing some passages of Scripture that remind you how God empowers you to overcome.

If I know God is all knowing, when my mind dwells on sinful thoughts, I will respond <u>by taking my thoughts captive *(2 Corinthians 10:5)* and by focusing instead on the things that are pure, noble, honorable, good, righteous, excellent, praiseworthy *(Philippians 4:8)*.</u>

If I know God is always present, when I face temptation, I will respond by _____

_____

_____

If I know God is all-knowing, when I feel overwhelmed and uncertain, I will respond by _____

_____

_____

If I know that God is all-loving, when I fail, I will respond by

_____

_____

If I know God is all-powerful, when I am facing an impossible situation, I will respond by _____

_____

_____

Action Steps for this chapter:

- Write new "I will" statements in your chapter journal. What will you do today and this week in response to God's voice?

- Complete the additional study for this chapter on God and His attributes.

- Share the truths you learn about God and His love in the additional study with someone who needs to hear them.

- **Memorize** *John 3:16* or *Titus 3:4-5.*

- Continue sharing your story and God's story with those on your list. Be ready to report back on what happened.

Chapter Journal

I will: _____

_____

_____

I will: _____

_____

_____

I will: _____

_____

_____

I will: _____

_____

_____

Notes:

_____

_____

_____

_____

_____

Additional study for this chapter:

Worship God and meditate on Him. Focus on the different aspects of His greatness!

- Read **Psalm 139.** Notice the attributes of God and how it led David to ask God to search his heart and confess his sins. Ask God to search your thoughts, attitudes, speech, and relationships. Confess any sins and be sure to forsake any sins that God reveals.
- Give thanks to Him for past, present, and future blessings.
- Praise God for who He is (His attributes and names)!
- Practice living each moment of the day with the intimate awareness that God is with you! Practice this by "praying without ceasing"!
- Pray for the development of your character and holiness. Pray for ministry opportunities. Reflect on and pray through the Scriptures. What is God saying to you? What must you do in response and obedience?

Chapter 10 Trainer's Guide
Life in the Church

Training Goal (Heartbeat): Encourage every disciple maker to commit to living on mission and participating in a local body of believers.

Expected Outcome (Skill/Habit): Every disciple maker will become an active participant in a local body of believers who are committed to the purposes of Christ and His Church.

 ## Look Back

Give everyone a chance to share, hear from others, and be held accountable. Focus on encouragement, celebration, and following through with assignments.

- **Obedience:** Have <u>everyone</u> report back on how they shared their story, God's story, and followed through with their "I will" statements since the last training. (This can be done as a large group or in smaller groups). It is important not to move forward with Chapter 10 before you have put into practice what was learned in the previous chapter. Can anyone share the memory verse?
- **Review:** Go over the expected outcome and key principle from Chapter 9. Summarize the key points learned from the previous training.
- **Remind:** Training is for trainers. Do those being trained have anyone ready and willing to be trained through this book?

Before Looking Up, have at least two people practice sharing their story or God's story in front of the group.

 ## Look Up

This chapter explains the importance of life in the church. As you train those you are discipling through this chapter, be sure to focus on these key concepts:

- Train in a way that every disciple understands the purpose of Christ and His Church as new churches are being planted.

- Remember to highlight the expected outcome and key principle! Encourage memorization of key Scripture verses. Did you memorize *John 3:16* or *Titus 3:4-5?*
- **Hearing from God:** At the end of this chapter, allow for a time of silent prayer and reflection, specifically looking for what each person should do in response to God speaking to their heart.

Group Discussion: Evaluate the 5 Fingers and discuss the importance of being connected to a church. Review the privileges and responsibilities of the church.

Model & Practice: Model how to encourage discipleship and active participation in a local body of believers by specifically addressing the ways they have seen two or three people grow in the group over the course of the training.

Look Forward

Before reviewing the action steps for the chapter, pause and prayerfully discuss the following questions:
- How is God speaking to your heart today?
- How is God calling you to greater obedience?
- What will you do in response to God's voice?

Action Steps for this chapter:
- Write new "I will" statements in your chapter journal. What will you do today and this week in response to God's voice?
- Follow the command of Jesus in baptism if you have not done so already.
- Begin or continue sacrificially giving.
- Begin or continue meeting together with those you have led to Christ. Encourage them to join your micro-church. Encourage them to obey the command of Christ and be baptized. For those willing and able, begin training them through this manual.
- Continue sharing your story and God's story with at least two to three people each week. By now it is becoming part of your lifestyle and is something you can continue without even needing to be reminded. The goal is to get to that point!

Chapter 10
Life in the Church

Expected Outcome: Every disciple maker will become an active participant in a local body of believers who are committed to the purposes of Christ and His Church.

When you become a Christian, you become a member of God's family. As covered in the last chapter, God is your Heavenly Father, and all followers of Jesus are your brothers and sisters. We are now part of the same family. In Christ, we are *"the house of God, which is the church of the living God" (1 Timothy 3:15).*

A household is not a building, and the Church is not a place or location of worship; the Church is a body of believers.

 Group Discussion: Read *Romans 12:5, Ephesians 1:22-23, and Ephesians 5:23.* From these passages, how does the Bible describe the relationship between Jesus and His followers?

 Key Principle: The Church is a spiritual family—with Christ in their midst as King—who loves God, loves others, and multiplies disciples.

The Church and Its Purpose in the World
Why did Jesus set up the Church, and how was it set up? There are five areas of church life that are important for every believer to know and understand. To help make this more memorable, we will illustrate these areas using our 5 fingers.

 ### One Purpose: Why does the Church exist?
The Church has one purpose: **To glorify God.**
The Church also has one Head: **Christ**
(Ephesians 1:22-23; 5:23).

Christ is the Head of the Church. There is no other. God has ordained only one *"Chief Shepherd" (1 Peter 5:1-4)*. Within the body of Christ, there is no hierarchy. *"The eye cannot say to the hand, 'I have no need of you'" (1 Corinthians 12:21)*. All parts work together for the good of the body. Each believer is a part of the body, and membership includes mutual accountability *(1 Corinthians 12:27)*.

Two Authorities: What guides the Church?
The Church has two authorities:
The Holy Spirit and the Holy Scriptures (Bible).

The Holy Spirit: God has provided His Spirit as a counselor and guide to each believer *(John 14:26)*. The Spirit **indwells** us at the point of salvation and guides/empowers us toward right thoughts and actions. When we sin, the Spirit brings conviction, leading us toward repentance and confession before God. His voice must be discerned as it guides the believer into God's will. The Spirit also **empowers** the believer for making disciples. He produces spiritual fruit and gives us spiritual gifts, which equip us to serve the Church and others towards maturity.

God's Word: To guide the Church, God appointed specific people throughout history under the leading of the Holy Spirit to record His instruction and plan for mankind. The Bible is without error and is the sufficient tool for discerning all matters of faith and practice. The Scriptures speak to all matters concerning the Church and must be central in the decision-making process of the body of Christ *(2 Timothy 3:16-17)*.

Together, the Spirit of God and the Word of God guide the Church. While the Spirit of God can speak apart from Scripture, there will never be a contradiction to the written Word of God. God's Spirit uses the Word as an instrument to instruct and, at times, correct the believer. The Word is the Spirit's way of shaping and directing the Church. Together, these two provide all that is needed for the Church to move forward in assurance of God's will. (For further study, see *Ephesians 5 and Colossians 3.*)

 Three Offices: Who should lead and what are their roles? The Church has three offices and many leaders.

1. Jesus, the Chief Elder/Shepherd *(1 Peter 5:1-4)*

2. Elders *(1 Timothy 3:1-7; Titus 1:5-9; Acts 14:23; 1 Peter 5:1-4)*
   - **Elder** is who they are.
   - **Overseer/Bishop** is what they do.
   - **Pastor/Shepherd** is how they do it.

3. Deacons/Servants *(Acts 6:3; 1 Timothy 3:8-13)*
   - Deacons serve the Lord by serving the church body.

 Group Discussion: Divide into two groups (one for elders and one for deacons) and read the verses above. Record the qualifications of those who serve and lead in a church. Have each group share what they find with everyone.

Elders	Deacons

Many well-intentioned followers of Jesus believe the pastors are the ones who should do the "work of ministry/service." A more careful reading of *Ephesians 4:11-12* reveals that the works of service are the responsibility and expectation of **every** believer.

Four Signs of Maturity: What are the characteristics of a maturing church? The church has four signs of maturity. As a church grows, it must take responsibility and ownership of each of these areas. This is comparable to the process of a child becoming an adult who is responsible for their actions and obligations.

1. **Self-Governing:** A church is mature enough to make decisions according to its two authorities: The Holy Scriptures and the Holy Spirit. (See *Acts 6:1-7* for an example.)

2. **Self-Multiplying:** A maturing church understands its role in evangelism and disciple making. Healthy things tend to grow, reproduce, and multiply. (Paul encouraged this in *1 Thessalonians 1:6-8.*)

3. **Self-Supporting:** A church takes responsibility and ownership for its activities, ministry outreach, and engagements. (See *Acts 2:44-45; 4:34-35* for examples of this.)

4. **Self-Correcting:** A proper understanding and application of the authorities in the church will lead to self-correcting behaviors. (See *2 Timothy 3:16-17* for examples of this.)

Five Practices: What are some practices of a healthy church body?

1. **Worship:** The expression of love toward God for His goodness, blessings, and faithfulness.
   "Praise the LORD! Sing to the LORD a new song, And His praise in the assembly of saints" (Psalm 149:1).

2. **Fellowship:** Loving the body of Christ and bearing one another's burdens.
   "And let us consider one another in order to stir up love and good works" (Hebrews 10:24).

148

3. **Discipleship:** Making disciples (including evangelism) and teaching them to obey everything Christ has commanded and ensuring this continues for multiple generations.
   "Go therefore and make disciples of all the nations, baptizing them in the name of the Father and of the Son and of the Holy Spirit, teaching them to observe all things that I have commanded you; and lo, I am with you always, even to the end of the age." (Matthew 28:19-20)

4. **Ministry:** Our works of service within the body through actions and attitudes.
   "For the equipping of the saints for the work of ministry, for edifying of the body of Christ ..." (Ephesians 4:12)

5. **Mission & Spirit-Filled Living:** When we are filled with the Holy Spirit, we are compelled to share the hope of Jesus with others.
   "But you shall receive power when the Holy Spirit has come upon you; and you shall be witnesses to Me in Jerusalem, and in all Judea and Samaria, and to the end of the earth" (Acts 1:8).

 Key Principle: We make disciples by going, baptizing, and teaching others to obey ALL that Christ commanded us!

 Group Discussion: Consider the first church in *Acts 2:41-47*. How many of the five functions do you see at work in this body of believers?

Why should we be connected to a local body of believers?

- We need worship, fellowship, discipleship, mutual accountability, and encouragement.
- We need to obey God's command: *"Not forsaking the assembling of ourselves together, as is the manner of some, but exhorting one another, and so much the more as you see the Day approaching" (Hebrews 10:25).*
- We need to avoid departing from the truth of the Bible.

- We need to mentor and be encouraged. Mature Christians are able to mentor and teach the new believers. New believers, in turn, have excitement that is contagious to mature believers. We need both mature and new believers in the body of Christ!

Our Privileges and Responsibilities in the Church
Baptism is commanded by Jesus and is how we go public with our faith *(Matthew 28:19-20; Romans 6:1-14; Acts 2:41).*

- Baptism was the starting point of discipleship in the early church. It is a symbol of our faith and a critical part of making disciples *(Matthew 28:19-20).*

- Baptism is a proclamation and confirmation of our faith. Baptism is going public with our faith *(Acts 2:41).*

- The words and actions of baptism communicate to those present that we are raised to new life in Christ Jesus *(Romans 6:3).*

- We know and feel that we are freed from the old dead person, and now live a new life in resurrection power *(Romans 6:4–5).*

- Baptism does not have the power to forgive sin. We are saved when we confess with our mouth and believe in our heart *(Romans 10:9)*

The Lord's Supper (communion) is commanded by Jesus and is how we celebrate and remember His sacrifice.

- Jesus personally established communion as a remembrance of His death and shed blood for our sin *(Matthew 26:17-19, 26-30).*

- When we receive the Lord's Supper, we remember and give thanks *(Isaiah 53:5).*

150

- The Lord's Supper is a time to self-examine our actions and faith *(1 Corinthians 11:23-29)*.
- The Lord's Supper is a time to pray and reflect on His life, death, and resurrection *(John 15-17)*.

Sacrificial giving is one way we show love and obedience to Jesus' command to love God and love others.
- Giving can include sacrifices of a person's life, goals, time, abilities, and finances.

- Sacrificial giving is required by God and is a test of the disciple's faith, love, and obedience.

- God commanded His people in the Old Testament to tithe, telling them the tithe belongs to God. Tithe means 10% *(Leviticus 27:30-31; Malachi 3:8-9)*.

- Sacrificial giving originates from a thankful and sincere heart. It is motivated by love and given according to what a person has and according to the needs of others *(2 Corinthians 8:9-15)*. We cannot worship God without gifts and offerings *(Acts 2:45; 2 Corinthians 9:7)*.

Model & Practice: Growth & Discipleship

In this chapter, we have learned how essential it is for the disciple maker to be part of a community of other believers to invest in, encourage, and challenge one another. The trainer will now model how to encourage discipleship by specifically addressing the ways they have seen two or three people grow in the group over the course of the training.

Group Discussion: Choose someone you want to celebrate in the group and share how you have seen them grow during the course of this training and share it with the group. Some of these areas of growth could be any of the following:
- Daily Devotions
- Spirit-filled living
- Sharing your story

151

- Sharing God's story
- Intentionally discipling others (new believers you led to Christ)
- Prayer

Group Activity: As people are describing the ways they have seen others grow throughout the training, pass your book around (or a paper with your name at the top) where people can write down one or two characteristics they have seen in each person.

_____

_____

_____

_____

_____

_____

_____

Now that you have heard some of the ways you have grown during the training, spend time in prayer and invite the Holy Spirit to prepare you to grow in other areas. Take time to write down these areas and then ask your trainer when you could meet to specifically assess your growth, development, and discipleship progress. Discuss how you can improve and make a plan to become a disciple who is worth multiplying.

It is also good to consider what fruit has come from this training and the plans that need to be made going forward. *Disciples Making Disciples - Level 2* may be an option for some.

Action Steps for this chapter:

- Write new "I will" statements in your chapter journal. What will you do today and this week in response to God's voice?

- Follow the command of Jesus in baptism if you have not done so already.

- Begin or continue sacrificially giving.

- Begin or continue meeting together with those you have led to Christ. Encourage them to join your micro-church. Encourage them to obey the command of Christ and be baptized. For those willing and able, begin training them through this manual.

- Continue sharing your story and God's story with at least two to three people each week. By now, it is becoming part of your lifestyle and is something you can continue without even needing to be reminded. The goal is to get to that point!

Chapter Journal

I will: _____

_____

_____

I will: _____

_____

_____

I will: _____

_____

_____

I will: _____

_____

_____

Notes:

_____

_____

_____

_____

_____

What's Next?

Now that you have completed *Disciples Making Disciples - Level 1,* you have new believers you are investing in to become disciple makers. If you have not done so already, you must quickly decide how to move this group of new believers into disciples who make disciples. There are a few ways to go forward in the disciple making relationship.

You can start a Discovery Bible Study to invite those you are sharing with and praying for to come to Christ. You can begin gathering with new believers on a regular basis as a smaller spiritual family under the banner and leadership of your existing church. While you remain aligned to the common vision, mission, and leadership of your existing church, this group of new believers can meet together in homes, offices, clubhouses, coffee shops, barber shops, etc.

- When you gather, we recommend you fellowship, study the Scriptures, pray, and serve both inside and outside the group in an effort to make disciples who make disciples. Remember the five practices of the church in Chapter 9.

- We recommend you continue to invest in your relationship with your Training Center and begin going through *Disciples Making Disciples - Level 2.* This will greatly assist you as you go forward in your discipleship journey and provide a guide and framework for developing your new and growing spiritual family into reproducing disciple makers.

Alternatively, you may choose to continue to disciple new believers as members of an existing church.

Discipling New Believers

The following pages cover the main points from each chapter of this book. It serves as a field guide to help new believers become disciple makers.

The chapter summaries are a simple model to follow when you meet together. The goals for new believers are a simple way to highlight and track the progress of the disciple making process.

We recommend you frequently meet with your new believers and encourage simple, loving, childlike obedience to Christ! You can also help them immediately identify people in their life with whom they can share the Gospel (just like you did with them).

Disciple Making Goals for New Believers		
	Yes	Not Yet
Baptism		
Spiritual fruit		
Understanding identity in Christ		
Obedience to Scripture		
Spirit-filled living		
Daily devotions and "self-feeding"		
Comfortable sharing "My Story"		
Comfortable sharing "God's Story"		
Training others		
Prayer walking		
Involved in a local church or DBS Group		
Sacrificial giving		

Chapter Summaries

As you go throughout the training to become a disciple who makes disciples, you will begin to make disciples! The lessons and principles that you are learning in your training must be passed on to the next generation of disciple makers.

While you may not feel prepared to train others through this book, it is essential that you begin training those who have made a decision to follow Christ. **Remember: All training is for trainers.**

The following pages contain the same training goals, expected outcomes, and Model & Practice lessons you have seen throughout your own training. In order to give those you are training a solid foundation of knowledge and application, summaries of the main teaching points and key action steps are also included. Go through these chapter summaries as you begin to train new believers to become disciples who make disciples.

Chapter 1 – The Spirit-Filled Christian Life

Training Goal: The goal of the trainer is to instill in every disciple maker a passion to daily pursue a Spirit-filled life (untying and raising their sails).

Expected Outcome: Every disciple maker will experience a Spirit-filled life (untying and raising their sails daily).

Model & Practice: Demonstrate how to untie and raise your sails. Share a specific example of when God used a small act of faith (raising their sail) to bring about an amazing encounter with someone who was being drawn to Jesus.

Key Principle: God the Father is constantly drawing people to Jesus through the ministry of the Holy Spirit. He <u>invites</u> and <u>expects</u> us to join Him in that process.

Key Scriptures:

1. **Jesus sent the Holy Spirit for our benefit** *(John 14:16-17).*

2. **We are to be filled with the Holy Spirit** *(Ephesians 5:18).*

3. **The Holy Spirit helps us tell others about Jesus** *(Acts 1:8).*

Action Step: Begin each day asking the Holy Spirit to fill you and take control of your life. You may need to ask Him to fill you multiple times throughout the day.

Chapter 2 – My Story

Training Goal: The goal of the trainer is to equip and motivate every disciple maker to recognize and respond in obedience to the opportunities God gives them to share their story. (The harvest is plentiful.)

Expected Outcome: Every disciple maker will regularly share their story of how Jesus changed their life with people where they live, work, study, shop, and play.

Model & Practice: Demonstrate how to share the story of how Jesus changed their life. Show how to start a spiritual conversation using questions and "defining moments." Everyone else should also practice writing and telling their story, both individually and in small groups. Give everyone a chance to share!

Your story is unique and a powerful way to tell others about Jesus. Usually a story has three parts:
1. What my life was like before I believed in Christ.

2. How I came to know Christ.

3. How my life has changed after knowing Christ.

Key Principle: Every believer is a disciple, and every disciple is called to be a disciple maker.

Key Scriptures:
1. **Every believer is called to make disciples** *(Matthew 28:19-20)*.

2. **Every believer is called to love God and love others** *(Matthew 22:34-40)*.

Action Step: Share your story with one person on your list or a pre-Christian this week.

Chapter 3 — God's Story

Training Goal: The goal of the trainer is to equip and empower every disciple maker to effectively share God's story.

Expected Outcome: Every disciple maker will make disciples by regularly sharing God's story where they live, work, study, shop, and play.

Model & Practice: Present the Gospel by sharing God's story using the 3 Circles and the Bridge Illustration. Show how to master three crucial transitions to leading someone to Christ.

God's story is sometimes called the Gospel. It tells how to have a relationship with God through His Son, Jesus.

Key Principle: God loved the world so much that He sent His Son, Jesus, so that those who believe in Him will receive eternal life *(John 3:16).*

Key Scriptures:
1. *"For all have sinned and fall short of the glory of God"* (Romans 3:23).
2. *"But God demonstrates His own love toward us, in that while we were still sinners, Christ died for us"* (Romans 5:8).
3. *"If you confess with your mouth the Lord Jesus and believe in your heart that God has raised Him from the dead, you will be saved"* (Romans 10:9).

Action Step: Share God's story with one person on your list or a pre-Christian.

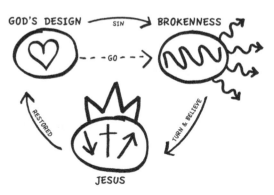

Chapter 4 – New Identity and Assurance of Salvation

Training Goal: The goal of the trainer is to provide every disciple maker with a biblical perspective of their identity in Christ and how to see themselves as God sees them.

Expected Outcome: Every disciple maker will stand firm in the assurance of their salvation; that Christ alone is enough.

Model & Practice: Give personal examples of how you have overcome temptations, failures, fears, and hardships as a result of understanding your new identity in Christ.

Key Principle: If you have trusted Jesus to be your Savior and Lord, then you have received eternal life! You are a Kingdom citizen! Your service to the King starts here and now!

Key Scriptures:

1. **The path to eternal life is through Jesus** *(1 John 5:11-13).*

2. **Faith in Jesus is the way of salvation** *(John 14:6).*

3. **Your new identity** *(2 Corinthians 5:17).*

4. **Your assurance of salvation** *(1 John 1:7-9).*

Action Step: Try to memorize at least one of the key Scriptures.

Chapter 5 – Living a Life of Prayer

Training Goal: The goal of the trainer is to inspire every disciple maker to passionately pursue a deeper relationship with God by making prayer a priority throughout their day.

Expected Outcome: Every disciple maker will experience a healthy prayer life directed by the Holy Spirit and God's Word.

Model & Practice: Demonstrate how to use the prayer wheel as a model for personal daily prayer time.

Prayer is "talking" with God, "listening" to God, and "hearing" from God. Jesus gave a simple example to follow when we pray.

Key Principle: Listen and talk to God throughout the day *(1 Thessalonians 5: 16-18)*.

Key Scripture: The Lord's Prayer *(Matthew 6:9-13)*
1. **Talk to God like a child would with their Father** *(Matthew 6:9)*.
2. **Worship and praise Him** *(Matthew 6:9)*.
3. **Pray for Jesus to set the world right and return soon** *(Matthew 6:10)*.
4. **Focus on advancing His Kingdom** *(Matthew 6:10)*.
5. **Ask Him to lead and be the Master of your life** *(Matthew 6:10)*.
6. **Ask Him to meet your needs and those of others you know** *(Matthew 6:11)*.
7. **Confess your sins to Him and forgive those you have not forgiven** *(Matthew 6:12)*.
8. **Ask Him for protection and victory over temptation and sin** *(Matthew 6:13)*.

Action Step: Pray the Lord's Prayer 7 minutes a day, 7 days a week, for 7 people.

Chapter 6 – Daily Devotions

Training Goal: The goal of the trainer is to foster a hunger in every disciple maker for studying God's Word, being able to better discern His voice, and applying it to their life.

Expected Outcome: Every disciple maker will faithfully read and study God's Word to better discern His voice and have the courage to obey whatever God says.

Model & Practice: Model how to do a personal Bible study so everyone sees how to do it. Practice together.

To really know a person, you need to have regular contact. If you want to have a close relationship with God, it is helpful to set a time **just for God** each day—this is called daily devotions.

Key Principle: The main purpose of daily devotions is to know and worship God and respond in obedience to what His Word and Spirit say.

Key Scriptures:

1. **Pursue God as a priority in your life** *(Matthew 6:33).*

2. **Trust in God and rely on Him to lead you** *(Proverbs 3:5-6).*

Action Step: Identify a consistent and specific time and place for daily devotions. Who will keep you accountable? Download the YouVersion Bible App, and identify a Bible reading plan.

Chapter 7 – Learning to Feed Yourself

Training Goal: The goal of the trainer is to show every disciple maker how to create a daily routine of spending time in God's Word, hearing His voice, and immediately obeying what He spoke.

Expected Outcome: Every disciple maker will set aside time every day to spend with God that includes the reading of His Word, prayer, and responding in obedience.

Model & Practice: Model how they do their own daily devotions. Encourage those you disciple to practice this week.

A newborn baby relies on his mother to be fed but must eventually learn to feed himself. In the same way, Christians must learn to feed themselves. This can be done through personal Bible study.

Key Principle & Scripture: Every believer must learn to grow in their understanding, trust, and obedience of God's Word *(2 Timothy 3:16)*.

1. **Scripture:** Copy the passage word-for-word exactly how it is written in the Bible.

2. **My Own Words:** Rewrite the passage in your own words.

3. **I Will:** Ask the Holy Spirit to reveal things you need to add to your life, take away from your life, or change in your life to obey this passage. **Be specific!**

4. **Prayer & Share:** Prayerfully reflect on who needs to hear the truths God has revealed to you. Share your "I will" statements and hold each other accountable. Look for opportunities to share what God said with others.

Action Step: Each day practice the personal Bible study method. Follow through with all of your "I will" statements and share with one person on your list or a pre-Christian.

Chapter 8 – Discovering the Bible

Training Goal: The goal of the trainer is to explain the value of training the next generation by equipping every disciple maker to confidently lead a Discovery Bible Study.

Expected Outcome: Every disciple maker will gather a group of new believers or "pre-Christians" to lead them through a Discovery Bible Study so they can begin to read God's Word, hear His voice, and respond in obedience.

Model & Practice: Model how to lead a Group Discovery Bible Study. Encourage those you disciple to practice leading one this week.

Discovery Bible Study is a simple, yet effective, method for reading and studying the Bible in a group context. By using the DBS method, Christians and pre-Christians can read the Scriptures together to learn about God and His character.

Discovery Bible Study prioritizes the reading of Scripture and discussion around guided questions that get to the heart of the passage and encourage practical obedience and life change. As the process is guided by the leading of the Holy Spirit, we are given every opportunity to hear what God actually wants to communicate to us.

Key Principle: By participating in a Discovery Bible Study, we can grow in our relationship with God and be mutually encouraged by the body of Christ.

Key Scripture:

The Word of God is living and active *(Hebrews 4:12).*

Action Steps: Prayerfully consider starting a Discovery Bible Study. If you start a Discovery Bible Study, invite anyone with whom you share your story or God's story. Talk with someone else in your Training Center about starting a group and then multiplying later as the group grows.

Chapter 9 – God Our Heavenly Father

Training Goal: The goal of the trainer is to help every disciple maker have a biblical understanding of God and how they can best respond to every situation in their life.

Expected Outcome: Every disciple maker will make decisions and choices informed by a biblical understanding of who God is and what He is like.

Model & Practice: Take time to explain how a biblical understanding of who God is and His attributes affect how the disciple maker will respond to different situations and circumstances in life.

Key Principle: God is your Heavenly Father and loves you unconditionally.

God is:
1. **Omnipotent**: all-powerful.
2. **Omnipresent**: always present/able to be everywhere at the same time.
3. **Omniscient**: all-knowing.
4. **Omnibenevolent**: all-loving.

Our Heavenly Father:
1. **Our Heavenly Father loves** *(Romans 5:8).*
2. **Our Heavenly Father protects** *(2 Kings 6:15-18).*
3. **Our Heavenly Father provides** *(Philippians 4:19).*
4. **Our Heavenly Father disciplines** *(Hebrews 12:6-7).*

Action Step: Share about your Heavenly Father and His love with one person on your list or a pre-Christian this week.

Chapter 10 – Life in the Church

Training Goal: The goal of the trainer is to encourage every disciple maker to commit to living on mission and participating in a local body of believers.

Expected Outcome: Every disciple maker will become an active participant in a local body of believers who are committed to the purposes of Christ and His Church.

Model & Practice: Model how to encourage discipleship and active participation in a local body of believers by specifically addressing the ways they have seen two or three people grow in the group over the course of the training.

Key Principle: A spiritual family—with Christ in their midst as King—loves God, loves others, and multiplies disciples.

Key Scriptures:

1. **Baptism is commanded by Jesus and is how we go public with our faith** *(Matthew 28:19-20; Romans 6:1-14; Acts 2:41).*

2. **The Lord's Supper (communion) is commanded by Jesus and is how we celebrate and remember His sacrifice** *(Matthew 26:17-19, 26-30).*

3. **Sacrificial giving is one way we show love and obedience to Jesus' command to love God and love others** *(Acts 2:42-47; 2 Corinthians 9:7).*

Action Step: Join a local body of believers, and experience baptism if you have not already been baptized. Begin or continue taking the Lord's Supper and giving.

TTI USA Training Materials Printed by:

Action Printech
Plymouth, MI
actionprintech.com

If you are interested in printing books or resources for your ministry, please contact **chris@actionprintech.com**

Made in the USA
Middletown, DE
20 September 2021